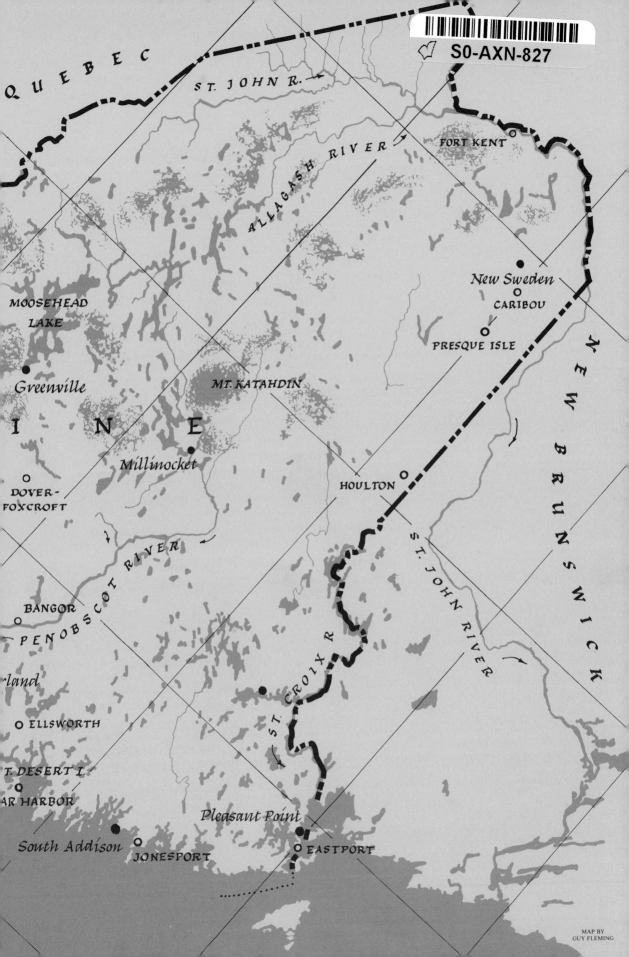

QUEBEC

ST. JOHN R.

FORT KENT

ALLAGASH RIVER

New Sweden
CARIBOU

PRESQUE ISLE

MOOSEHEAD
LAKE

NEW BRUNSWICK

Greenville

I   N   E

MT. KATAHDIN

Millinocket

DOVER-
FOXCROFT

HOULTON

ST. JOHN RIVER

PENOBSCOT RIVER

BANGOR

ST. CROIX R.

land

ELLSWORTH

T. DESERT I.

AR HARBOR

Pleasant Point

South Addison

JONESPORT

EASTPORT

MAP BY
GUY FLEMING

THE VOICE OF
MAINE

THE VOICE OF

MAINE

WILLIAM L. POHL,

with photographs by

ABBIE SEWALL

THORNDIKE PRESS

Thorndike, Maine

Library of Congress Cataloging in Publication Data:

Pohl, William L., 1955-
  The voice of Maine.

  1. Maine – Biography. 2. Maine – Social life and
customs. 3. Interviews – Maine. I. Title.
CT238.P63   1983   974.1'043'0922   83-10564
ISBN 0-89621-075-8

Cover photograph by Abbie Sewall.

Book and cover design by Guy Fleming.

Editing by Abby Trudeau.

Photocomposition by The Comp Shop.

Second printing, 1984.

Contents

Introduction

In THE VOICE OF MAINE, William Pohl and Abbie Sewall present us with a picture of contemporary Maine through a series of written and photographic snapshots. Pohl and Sewall have succeeded because of their choice of subjects, because of their ability in getting interviews with people indisposed to such things, and because they have allowed each subject to paint his own portrait. Their collaboration with each subject is both biographical and autobiographical; even the composition of each photograph seems to grow out of the subject's own life world.

When these portraits are brought together, they overlap, amplify, and reflect each other to produce a larger portrait of a whole people. These people, the Maine people, in a mysterious way speak with one voice that Pohl and Sewall could not possibly have engineered.

This is the voice of Maine, the vanguard of a new America, so new and fresh precisely because it has grounded itself so solidly in the old. Let me not be too chauvinistic about Maine. It is surely one of the most hidebound states in the Union. Nevertheless, Maine is showing the way to true modernity through tradition, and this new consciousness is emerging everywhere.

MARSHALL DODGE III

Portland, Maine
1980

Foreword

AGAIN AND AGAIN in his autobiographical reflections, William Carlos Williams remarked upon the nourishing connection between observable reality and the mind's imaginative life. He admonished those writers he knew or corresponded with to keep eyes and ears open, no matter how "private" their property or novels; "I don't go for the distinction as I hear it proclaimed by a lot of academics." He was admonishing a medical student, interested in doing a bit of writing, to make a few more connections, to let go of a few well-memorized classifications and categorizations.

Books such as this surely would have pleased the "old Doc Williams" (as his patients called him) I was lucky to know. He had fast-moving, alert, responsive eyes, and they would have enjoyed the sight of these ordinary, unpretentious, hardworking men and women. He had eager, attentive ears, and they would have delighted in hearing the voices offered them, at a remove, on these pages. Once he told me, "Sometimes, when I read a good conversation, I hear it — the words go through my head in such a way that they make noise." Maine people are, by and large, quiet, if not reticent. Still, they can be persuaded to say a few rather interesting and important things, as this book convincingly demonstrates, and so a New Jersey poet would no doubt have loved the noise in his head if he had been around to let himself get carried north a few hundred miles into a quite distinctive world.

The eminent virtue of this collaborative effort is a persistent modesty altogether in keeping with the "subject matter" — if one may, ironically, get abstract about the lives of particular human beings. Maine is, one begins to realize, not only a state, but a state of mind — a social and cultural setting with enough persuasive authority to exert a continuing influence on generation after generation of inhabitants. And the thrust of that influence tends toward a reserve, a subdued but adroit and wry watchfulness, a contemplative and bemused kind of personal independence. These are sturdy but not self-important or expansively active people. They go about their business, do their work, live their lives, scratch their heads, smile, but make no big deal about this and that — the "causes", one after the next, that preoccupy some of us noisier, more prepossessing people. Nor is the issue only one of stoicism, or political conservatism. These are often enough vulnerable, hard-pressed individuals. Maine is a rather poor state. Its citizens must contend all the time with substantial difficulties. A certain kind of populist reformer might well make hay in the state — were he or she able to connect activist politics to a social climate that insists upon restraint, tact, a never-ending respect for tradition as well as a person's right to privacy.

If we Americans are to get to know each other better — learn to understand our particularity, our diversity — we will need, for state after state, and for all our regions, books such as this: careful, sensitive, respectful responses (assisted by those familiar twentieth-century artifacts, the camera and the tape recorder) to the *ways* of people, to their visual presence and their heartfelt, spoken sentiments. Our universities, our foundations, the cultural institutions maintained by our federal and state governments, would do well to pay heed, to see this book as an exemplary instance of what a democracy craves if it is to stay alive and well: a constantly re-examined social consciousness.

ROBERT COLES, Harvard University

Cambridge, Massachusetts

THE VOICE OF

MAINE

LAURA RIDGEWELL

West Point

ONE RECENT FEBRUARY, *a hurricane-force Nor'easter slammed into shore, burying Manhattan, Providence, and Boston under two feet of snow. Emergencies were declared.*

The storm caught everyone by surprise. Snow was not content to flutter gently for the convenience of municipal plowers. This snow was hard core, swirling in thick flaws and eddies. Light was smothered between dusky canyons of glass and concrete. Winds banked drifts over streets, and commuters were stranded.

Business ground to a muffled halt as people came out of windowless offices, tenements, and stores to watch their cities undergo transformation. Humdrum grays, sooty blacks, and industrial yellows were blanketed by a coat of ozone-laden white. Everything glistened in pools of light beneath the street lamps. The clanking, honking, hustling, grinding, wailing, grating of a trillion unnatural distractions quieted. The bubbub of the restless masses hushed.

This unheard-of eerie silence created the usual anxieties in people, of course. It also conjured feelings of human recognition that momentarily defied the anonymity of life in the cities. People broke out of lonely shells to commiserate, share food, shrug their shoulders. Neighbors became neighborly. Strangers in candlelit bars and subways exchanged stories of blizzards and blackouts past. The storm was almost a festive occasion, an excuse to be human again, brought on by the simple intrusion of snow.

Then the spell began to break. The National Guard was called in to clear airport runways. Highways were plowed. Snow was carted away. Smog replaced sparkle; soot reclaimed the sidewalks. The pace of life quickened, and dreary routine set in. City people breathed an enormous sigh of relief. The emergency was over.

[3

The Nor'easter also battered the coast of Maine. Churning gray-green waves swept in on a full moon high tide that ripped fishing boats from moorings and swept docks out to sea. Streets flooded, and roofs were torn apart. Yet in Maine, no emergency was declared.

After the storm Mainers helped each other muddle through life much as they did before. They grumbled, picked up the pieces, and nailed their lives back together with recycled wood. Their quiet confidence never wavered. Storms had become a part of their existence; they were stoically endured.

When the wind and waves died down, Laura Ridgewell took time to describe how she rode out the tempest in West Point, the fishing village where she lives.

Ridgewell is a mountain of energy, a can-do woman not content to sit on her thumbs whistling for a wind. Dressed in a checkered lumber jacket and jeans, she wipes a tangle of hair off her forehead with the back of her hand and attends to coffee and a pot-helion boiling on the stove. She tells what it's like to be the wife of a Down East fisherman.

LAURA RIDGEWELL / *West Point*

"WEST POINT IS ALL FISHERMEN. When I get up in the morning, the first thing I smell is low tide kelp and rotten bait. Tourists go around saying, 'Hummmm, the air is so invigorating.' Ugh. I have tears in my eyes, the bait smell is so heavy in the air.

"Each morning I hear boat engines. I know everyone by sound from my bedroom window. The diesel sound is normally a mellow, whirring sound that purrs like a cat. There aren't many boats like that in our harbor. Most boats here are converted automobile engines with crummy exhaust systems that consist of a pipe up through the roof. Old one-lungers — when you start them up, they rag and bleat, loud and piercing, like some dying animal.

"The sounds of engines are important. When I hear the engine of our boat, I know my husband is coming, and everything is all right. When I don't hear his engine, I know he's not coming — maybe for several days and nights until he can fetch a good catch. Maybe never.

"We listen for the boat engines and get to know everyone by sound. I say, 'There goes Frederick York. That's Eugene Atwood. Here comes Philip Wyman.' All from the bedroom window. This knowledge creeps up on us unawares.

"For the fishermen at sea, engine sounds are important. They can fall asleep to those sounds. The noise is a security blanket that says all is well. Engines that suddenly go quiet spell trouble.

"The sound of wind is also important, especially when we know that it's going to take away all of the things that we have worked so hard for. No fisherman that I know has ever put in for a loan to pay for storm damage. Instead, they scrounge. If they lost a pier, they'll push off to the islands to salvage the pieces. Like they've done before. Like Nort Wallace is doing now.

"When I can't understand something, I'm afraid. I don't understand politics. We don't know what the politicians want, and it seems that they don't care about our needs.

"We weren't qualified for loans after the storms of 1978. Even though West Point was a disaster area, the government said that the storm was at Wells Beach and other summer resorts. Fishermen who lack political influence 'didn't have a storm.'

"We're lucky. We 'didn't have a storm.' But I wish somebody told me we didn't have a storm when the winds here were gusting over 80 knots, and I couldn't see out the window because of all of the sand, mud, and salt. The pickup trucks in front of the house were up to here in tide. At night I lay on my bed and felt the whole house shake in the gale. The sound of wind blotted out all other sounds.

"Fishermen are different. We respect the ocean. We don't run up to the surf on the beach and say, 'Get me if you can.' We don't do that. We take a boat out there and know that in one-half hour's time, the living-room-floor-calm of the ocean can turn into a squall from which we might never return. We see a storm coming, and we get to the lee of an island. When I hear the sound of wind, Bob, my husband, says, 'Don't worry, Laura.' Well how can I not worry when the ice starts to form on the riggin', masthead, and railing turning the entire boat white. When the ice topsides gets heavier than the keel, the boat capsizes. Last year a scallop boat went out and never returned. Bob was out then too.

"So we look out after ourselves. We can't depend on the government for help. We don't call upon the government for welfare. We call upon our neighbors. If someone is ill, we share food, take care of their kids, and help out. We're natural survivors.

"I see things differently too. Like Popham Beach up the road. Tourists love it in the summer, but to me, you can't see the sand because of all of the umbrellas and picnic wrappings. My beach is a fish wharf. When I jump off, it's just me, the eels and the pollack. The only pollution is what the gulls leave behind.

"I also like to see the loons in the fog, moose swimming out to the islands, whales spouting in the bay, and the seals in the cove. Which reminds me of the time I got my head stuck up a culvert. I was walking home from school in my Sunday best and saw some frog's eggs in a culvert. I took off my hat, my heels and gloves and left them by the side of the road. Then I waded into the mud to look for tadpoles.

"The school superintendent was driving by and came upon my stuff. He stopped the car and ran into the culvert saying, 'Mrs. Ridgewell, can I help you?'

"I was busy. Without looking up, I said, 'No, not unless you've got a fish net or something. I'm trying to catch frog eggs.'

"Well, he let out a sigh of relief and said, 'Oh, I thought you were trying to commit suicide in the pond.' He was in a suit, and I was in my white dress, covered with mud. I had a circle of dirt around my eye from looking through a reed at the eggs. A real mess.

"Now people know me. I can stick my eye up a culvert, and people just drive by and wave. That's why I like living here at West Point.

"What else do I see? Everything that's important to me. I don't see cars or clothes hanging out to dry. I don't see poverty or severe winters or hardship. I don't see 'going back to nature.' I've already been there and don't notice those things.

"I also don't see women's liberation. My father was a fisherman who had the misfortune to have four daughters and no son. He may have been slightly annoyed, but never mentioned it to us.

"We'd go out fishing and bait the needles and steer the boat while he hauled the lobster pots. When he wasn't looking, we'd play with seahorses and starfish, and feed the bait to the seals and seagulls. Nothing boys would do.

"My father never got uptight about this. He just shrugged and said, 'Well, I guess we have to go in early today — the girls fed the bait to the seals.'

"Two years ago Bob broke his leg while jumping into the boat. He

couldn't work, and we didn't have enough money to live on except for $100-a-week workmen's compensation. That's not enough for a husband, a wife, and an 11-year-old son.

"I thought about this, and knew that I had to become a lobsterman 'till Bob recovered. That was a hell of a challenge for me. I had to stop being afraid that a lobster was going to attack me. I hate to pick up a lobster because when you think that they can't — they do.

"Nevertheless, I pushed off that week without my father, without Bob, and without pony-tails in my hair. I wasn't going to mess around with starfish or seals. I was going to captain my own boat out there for the money.

"I was petrified. I had to put on an oil slicker and gloves that were too big for my hands. I was scared of running somebody over in the boat. There's a lot of water between me and my small orange and black pot buoys. In getting to a buoy, the sea is moving, you're moving, and the buoy is bobbing. It took me a week before I could catch one. Then, I had to pull 50 heavy, water-soaked lobster traps by hand from the ocean floor in the cold every day into November. It was impossible.

"Meanwhile, you have to imagine what all of the old codgers were thinking as they stood on piers watching this woman out there chasing pot buoys. First of all, women are considered bad luck at sea. I was making circles counterclockwise around the traps which is also bad luck. Everytime I missed a buoy, I steamed a mile and a half around it before swinging back for another try. I spent more on gas that first week than I made from the entire catch.

"Soon I got the hang of it, but I never did get over one problem. When men measure how many fathoms it is to the ocean floor, they use a sounding line. Six feet of line is measured by holding the line out across one's chest with arms and hands extended as far as they'll go. Because of my bust, my fathoms were always bigger. The line floating above my traps was in danger of getting clogged in the propeller.

"Then, there was that bait smell again — ugh. I used to swim from boat to shore for my first bath, and then lemon my hands and soak in a tub. It never really goes away.

"Still, I was very popular with the men. They thought it was the funniest thing they'd ever seen, but they never made wisecracks. I was right up there with 'em. All they could see was another human being trying to survive. It wasn't a question of women's lib, and we kept ourselves off welfare while Bob was getting better.

[9

"You know, there is so much air between Laura Ridgewell and the President of the United States. He doesn't know that I sit up nights, waiting for a boat to come in.

"Our government wants us all to be the same. If we can't make a living, they put us on welfare and under their power. Is this place too good for the fishermen? Should all waterfront housing be reserved for doctors and lawyers? And yet the government is taxing the fishermen off the land of their ancestors.

"Bob Ridgewell is a fisherman. He is not a lawyer. Like other fishermen, he sings his song solo. The government must realize that we can't be made into a chorus. Fishermen must remain independent."

ALTON RAYNES

Owl's Head

In the mist *of the Grand Banks, the silhouette of a fisherman takes shape, gillnetting from the Narwhale. Gracefully the Friendship sloop comes into the wind, life spilling out of her sails. The fishermen hauls in his catch, straining and pulling on thinly woven nets. As herring break the glassy surface, their silvery underbellies cast blinding reflections. Alton Raynes wakes up with sun in his eyes. He has been dreaming as he sits in the rocking chair on the porch overlooking Owl's Head harbor.*

Years ago Raynes fished from the Narwhale before adapting to boats with diesel engines, mechanical winches, and radar. He speaks with a soft melodic lilt that trails off with memories. Staring into middle distance with heavy-lidded, half-closed eyes, his fingertips touch lightly, his mind far away. Old generations, new generations — the world is changing through the eyes of the fisherman as he sits rocking on the porch.

Alton Raynes / *Owl's Head*

"I was born in 1908. Grew up on a farm in Saint Georges across from Owl's Head. Didn't go to high school, but started right in with my father, milkin' cows and hayin'. I started a-fishin' when I was 10 years old, lobsterin' in winter and hook fishin' in summer. My father hauled the trawls, and I jogged the sloop, wound the buoy lines, and done the cookin'. And if I didn't do things just right, I'd hear about it.

[1 1

"We used to fish from sailboats and done everything by hand. It was natural. I still look over my terrace now and watch the sailboats. They're makin' 'em head-heavy after the racing boats, but they don't handle too well that way in a squall. In my *Narwhale*, she was well-balanced. She'd luff herself into the wind, spill her speed, and come onto her feet without my help. Gave me a chance to trawl in the halibut.

"I've been lobsterin' all my life. I got to learn their habits some. They'll come onto shore in summer, and go off in winter. You can chase 'em in and out, but you can't trap 'em when they're molting. They're cute. Make a nice lookin' trap, and you'll catch one. Make a funny lookin' trap, and it'll catch five. I guess they're curious.

"Back then we used to get up to nine halibut a day. We'd salt them. They dried up one-third; we'd get 300 pounds out of 1,000 pounds of wet fish. Then we'd sell them around North Haven, where the summer people was, for between one and eight cents a pound. Fish was cheap, and good bait could be had for three cents a pound.

"We used dories to haul the trawl. They're one of the ablest boats in the world. They have a flat bottom like a sea gull; they can set on the water in a gale, rising on the waves, but they'll never upset if trimmed right.

"To stabilize a boat in rough seas, we'd use sea anchors. They're open-ended cylinders attached to a line which you'd throw over the side. When a sea hit your boat, the water would drive through the sea anchor, yanking it against the motion of the wave. This softened the blow, and slowed the pitch and roll of the boat. In rough seas we'd 'back up' using the sea anchors, and half the crew would be seasick.

"We had no navigation gear in them days. Plenty of times I got stuck in fog and wouldn't know where I was. So I'd feel my way in to shore using a sounding lead attached to a hundred-fathom line.

"The sounding lead weighed 10 pounds, and we'd put soap or butter in a hole cut into its bottom. After we threw it over the rail, the butter would catch whatever was on the bottom. Black gravel at 70 fathoms was a sign of good fishing grounds. The fish often feed around the shoals. If you brought up mud in your lead, that was a sign of smaller fish like pollack (where we fished) which were worth less. Anyway, the lead tells you the depth of the water beneath your boat, and the kind of bottom you're over.

"To find where you are, you get out a nautical chart, take a sighting with the sun or stars, and compare your depth and bottom to what's on paper.

"If we was really lost and had to start from scratch, we'd set a buoy and sound around it. We'd go north 20 minutes, turn a square and go east 20 minutes, and do that all around the buoy as we heaved the lead and sounded for the bottom. Then we'd compare our findings over that square half-mile with the contours on the chart. If there was no other place like it on paper, we'd establish a position to some fixed point on shore and head for it. Nothin' sure about it, but most of the time we was dead right.

"To find bottom today, all you do is turn on a soundin' machine and watch the contour of the sea floor appear on the screen. It'll tell you fathoms, and where to fish. If you're lost, you get on the radio and ask someone where you are. It's a lot easier.

"One time I was fishin' off Vinalhaven, and a wicked bad storm come up on us fast. We only had time to catch three halibut when night caught up with us. Them seas was so bad, that I didn't even try to make for harbor.

"I put a sea anchor out and let her back up, and I sounded and got back 40 fathoms of water. I was lost, and noticed dirty yellow foam coming off some rocky ledges nearby. That scared me some for fear of runnin' aground.

"Then I saw a schooner. I recognized it as Capt'n Pickford comin' in from Boston bound for Vinalhaven. I decided to follow him in, even though he was on the leeward side of Treehaven and was close to foam comin' off the Matinicus Rock. He'd seen plenty of rough water before, and knew the routes better than I. He had decided to avoid the natural channel in due to the winds. He took the western bay where the channel was deepest, and we both made it in with my crew sick and layin' on the floor.

"I've seen other dirty weather. One year I was scalloping up to Provincetown. We decided to square-up and head for Owl's Head to put the boat up for winter. We picked up on a good breeze aimed sou'west straight for Monhegan Island. But this zephyr didn't die out like most sou'westers do. It hauled out sou'east and started to breeze up and rain. Them seas started breakin' on the side, and the old engine started skippin'. I didn't dare go out on the bow to luff in the sail 'cause it was real nasty out there. When the sail filled with water and bellied out, I tied a knife on a gaff pole and cut it, letting it tear to shreds in the wind.

"By morning the wind had died out some, but the sea was runnin' more and sheddin' a thin fog. I hauled up east a point for Bantam Buoy, and figured that in 16 miles I'd reach Old Man Whistler buoy in Owl's Head. Well 16 miles exactly I reached a lobster pot. Its markings belonged to B. Waton,

Byron Waton, and I knew him. I turned 'round to find myself right in the fairway safe from the ledges. It were 25 hours from the time I left Cape Cod — that were a pretty good long shot.

"I've been pretty cautious. I take plenty of extra gas and supplies, and I don't defy the elements. A ring around the moon comes; I know it means something. I didn't put it there. Somebody bigger than me did, so I go by it. It means a storm. If you count the stars inside that ring, they're days. Three stars in there tells you that the storm is three days away, roughly.

"The tide is also a forerunner of a storm. If it rips and a lot of rock and alewives are out, there's gonna be weather you'd best not be out in.

"Then there's sundogs. They're little pieces of rainbow north and south of the sun at dawn and dusk. If the sundog to the south is weak, and strong to the north — that signals an approaching nor'easter — bad weather.

"You hear other terms. 'Down East' refers to runnin' downwind east along the Maine coast towards Canada. Haulin' 'out south' means brailing in towards Provincetown. 'Upcountry' refers to flatlanders and mountains inland, and 'wet-landers' live on the shore. Boats are referred to as 'she,' and are named for women. Most women are 'she's' if they're lucky. Just a manner of speech.

"I've been cautious, but once in a while I get surprises. I was once fishin' around Stillwagon Bank in Buzzard's Bay and wanted to haul out to New Bedford to sell our scallops. We went through the Cape Cod canal to get there.

"Just going eight miles through that canal, and the whole world changed. The water on the other side was warmer, the fish was different, and the tide comes in four feet in Woods Hole instead of 12 feet in the Bay.

"I asked a fellow why the tide in Woods Hole only rose four feet. He said, 'That tide's so busy goin' to New York City that it don't have time to rise.' That must be the answer; it's caught in rush hour. Yes, sir."

H. FRANKLIN ORR

Orr's Island

A GREENHORN SAILOR *leaves harbor in a sailboat and finds himself fighting heavy currents and headwinds. Frustrated, he prays that the wind and current will be going in the other direction when he returns....*

H. Franklin Orr's stories were unbanishable like the "ayuh's" that punctured his speech. If the undercurrents of his humor were subtle, his voice was not. It sounded, fathoms deep, clear as a foghorn. People all over Orr's Island recognized that briny voice, the elemental nose, the playful eyes, and the weathered brow. They belonged to a man, tenacious as a barnacle on a mussel, who was born and died on the island of his ancestors.

H. FRANKLIN ORR / *Orr's Island*

"IT's always been a tradition on Orr's and Bailey Islands for the fishermen to start work early in the morning. In the old days my great-uncle used to start out anytime after midnight. He had a cow or two which he'd take with him down the field to pasture. Then he'd continue to shore, and throw his gear into a peapod dory. He'd row or sail out to the Cedar Ledges where he'd wait until there was light enough to see. There, he'd haul in his traps, and sail back. He said he got up so early so as to take advantage of the calmer water in early morning.

"My father was a fisherman. He was lost at sea in 1929, trawlin' in a February snowstorm. That was 16 years after I was born. Ayuh. Those were bad times, so I followed in his footsteps, starting in lobstering at age 13.

"I can remember the first lobster I ever caught. I was out in a dory with a friend of mine, and we caught one. We was so excited that instead of waitin' to catch another, we went back in to sell it right away. We got 45 cents for it. Since we used my friend's trap he got 25 cents for his share.

"When I wasn't lobsterin', I was clamming on the mud flats. Ayuh. It was backbreaking work. Lived with the tides, clammin' them in morning and at night.

"It was cold work. Unlike a fishing boat where you can warm your hands by placing them on the exhaust pipe, all we could do was to slap hands on opposite shoulders to keep the circulation going. We all had patches of mud on each shoulder by the end of the day, and our hands were raw and painful. All for $1.50 a barrel. Today clams fetch $96 a barrel.

"You can spot a clam by air holes in the sand. The critter has to breathe, so he'll squirt water out to keep that hole open as deep as three feet. You'd use a six-pronged haul for hard diggin' among rocks and gravel. For soft clay and mud, we used a long-pronged haul.

"We also used to dig longer for the bigger clams by the water's edge by mounding up mud with a squeegee — a board on a stick. That kept the sea from swashin' into the diggin' area. Ayuh.

"I also used to spudge for eels with a long, 12-foot pole. It has six barbed prongs. We'd spudge them out of the eel grass and mud. You'd know when you got one — they put up quite a fight, pushin' and shovin'. Ayuh. They had real fine teeth, but as long as you didn't pay any attention to them, neither did they. Eel was real good smoked.

"We used to sea-moss too, draggin' for it in the ocean. It used to be big business in Ireland, but they stopped importing it during the war due to the U-boats. That gave us a chance to make a livin' from it. Sea moss was processed into a gelatin mixture. It was used to make syrups and bases for soda and ice cream.

"You know, down through the years, fishermen had plenty of stories to tell. One of the best was Irving 'Scuppy' Dexter who lived down the road here. Once he told me about this Friendship sloop under full sail in Casco Bay that got sunk on a beautiful, clear day. He said that her sail caught a big migration of monarch butterflies, and that did her in.

"You know what a jig is? It's a baitless shiny hook that attracts codfish when you jiggle it. These codfish will eat anything shiny from false teeth to wristwatches. In jiggin', we'd set a line full of these hooks, and shake it. Sometimes we'd hook cods by the mouth, fins, and tails.

"Scuppy told about one fellow he knew who was wearing a vest to keep warm while jigging. It got warm, and he took the vest off. A breeze come along and puffed the vest topsides.

"According to Scuppy this fellow kept fishing, and caught a codfish. And do you know, that cod was wearing the vest.

"One other time Scuppy told me about a fellow who jumped on his fishing vessel and thought he recognized him. The man asked, 'Where in hell have I seen you before?'

"Without batting an eye, Scuppy asked the man what part of hell he came from."

CLAYTON *and*

WILLIAM JOHNSON

Bailey Island

DAWN AT MACKEREL COVE. *The only things visible through the fog are the red and green running lights of Clayton Johnson's fishing boat. It coughs bronchially, gasping for air and fuel as it thunks out of the harbor, shattering the morning stillness. Cutting a wake through the murky gloom, Clayton passes staysailed boats and rickety shanties on shore. Hearing the foghorn off Seguin, he knows to steer a wide course around the ledges by the Natural Steps. A quicksilver sun melts off the fog, leaving wispy trails of vapor that hang over the swells. "The finest kind of day," mutters Johnson as he circles a trap buoy.*

Clayton and William, his brother, are two of the Bailey Island Johnsons whose names adorn a string of dented mailboxes from the General Store to Land's End. At the tip of the island is a statue of Elroy Johnson, an earnest-looking man who was lost at sea. For decades the Johnsons have returned to Mackerel Cove with holds full of fish and wriggling blue shell and claw. "The finest kind of eating."

By noon Clayton is back. It is a clear pale-blue day, and one can see silvery Mount Washington and the Presidential Range from the rocks above the Cove. At sunset the sky prisms pink and mauve as cool ocean mists suffuse the island with the smell of salt and kelp. The moon begins to rise over the horizon, oversized and orange. Its light glows dimly on aluminum roofs and plays in the wind on swaying telephone wires. "The finest kind of views."

Some days are less candescent. Oily drizzle and dirty weather can move in for weeks. The Johnson brothers use this time in a patchwork quonset hut, resting in a neglected corner of the Cove on uncertain foundations. Surrounded in sepia light by a dismal web of gillnets, shards, and the paraphernalia of the fishing trade, the Johnson brothers darn gloves, chat about the weather, and nail up broken traps. "Fishin' can spoil you for anything else," Clayton says. "It's the finest kind of work."

C L A Y T O N   J O H N S O N   /   *Bailey Island*

"I WAS BORN IN 1908, and started fishing with my father, George Johnson, when they first come into having engines on the boats. We had an old five-horsepower Lathrope engine on ours. Even with all five-horses of her goin', we had to have a small boat and a small net 'cause there wasn't much power. It was a one-cylinder engine with a regular transmission and spark plugs. There was a first, second, and high gear. To get her going in reverse, we had to open her up full throttle.

"We used to go mackerel fishin' from June to October. We used a 70- by 90-foot square net which floated in high water. It was fastened to shore by a leader which we called the 'backbone.' This leader stretched from shore, 75 fathoms deep where it was anchored. Attached to the leader was a smaller four-inch-mesh net, weighted with rocks so it hung straight down. The schools of fish would follow the leader into the trap of our large net.

"We'd set our mackerel nets at dusk when they gilled, and return in a couple of hours to haul in our catch. Those mackerel would drive their heads into the mesh of the net, and get caught in the gills. We sold the fish for 50 cents-a-hundred. If we got two dollars a pound, we'd be lucky.

"The only thing I didn't like about fishin' was gettin' seasick. I didn't care whether I lived or died then, I got so sick. I used to climb up on the washboard and worry my father. Like most fishermen, none of us could swim. No one on Damariscove Island could ever teach me, and we all got to thinkin', 'What's the use — the water's too cold to survive in anyway.' The trick was not to fall in.

"We also used to go draggin' with 60-foot nets that we'd throw overboard. Washboards spread the net out behind the boat in your wake. Buoys

kept the top of the net afloat.

"When we dragged for bottom fish like haddock, flatfish, cod, hake, and red perch, we put rollers on the bottom of the net. They'd roll over rough, rocky bottoms. We also used to attach chains which dug into smooth muddy bottoms, scooping up flounder.

"When we went tuna fishin', we used harpoons that we tossed from the bow pulpit of the boat. Once you got the pike stuck in one of those fish, you'd let him take off with it as most things weighing 600 pounds are apt to do. There's no stoppin' a running tuna; he'll drag your boat behind him 'till he tires in about two hours. Then you haul him in. They've got to keep movin' forward in the water, or they drown. That's how you kill them, usually.

'I once caught 86 tuna in one year, some weighin' as much as 800 pounds. There was no market for them back then. Sometimes I had to cut them up for lobster bait 'cause I couldn't sell 'em. And I've sold tons of them for two cents a pound.

"Did you ever read Harold Clifford's book, *Charlie York – Maine Fisherman?* Me and my family used to live with him summers on Damariscove Island off Boothbay – a barren, grassy rock with a life savin' station on it. We got to know York real well. We stayed there only because it was nearer to fishin' grounds. In winter we all returned to our house on Bailey Island.

"Everybody liked York. He could speak real well, even though he never really got his words right. Both he and Elroy Johnson, whose statue is at Land's End, used to be called up to Augusta to speak before the state legislature on fishin' bills. They'd show up in their checkered guide shirts and fish-scaled boots, and the whole floor would go quiet. They spoke so well, you'd think they were senators.

"York was a funny man in some ways. He swayed between binges of Christianity and drinkin' – between the pulpit and the saloons. Once he went to California to appear on the Art Linkletter TV show. They had a guy like Houdini who boasted that he could get out of anything the audience could devise. He had gotten out of locked safes, handcuffs, and cages. Nothin' worked.

"Well, Charlie got up, still wearin' his boots, and asked if he could fasten on a few fishin' knots he knew. That escape artist never did get out of them knots. No, sir."

"I once had to rescue a man. A storm was breezin' up, so my grandson and I quit fishin' and knocked off early. We were just off Bailey Island when we saw that a boat had drifted ashore to the lee of the island. Somebody was wavin' an orange flag.

"We moved in closer and saw that a punt had upset, and this fellow was hangin' on to it. He weighed 350 pounds or more — oh what a big fellow he was. So we tied a rope around his arms and trunk and towed him off. The wind was blowin' onto the shore, and we was afraid of runnin' aground ourselves.

"We tried to get him in the boat, but he almost capsized us. I ripped the whole rear end of his pants out tryin' to pull him aboard. So finally, I got some fishin' tackle and fastened it around this fat man so that it would draw him up by the back, stomach downwards. Then we got his arms on the washboard, winched him up, and steamed back into harbor. My, he was a mighty big catch."

WILLIAM JOHNSON / *Bailey Island*

"I WAS BORN IN 1903, and have followed the water my whole life. I started out raking mussels from dories. They'd come in clusters all covered with mud. Us kids would come and pick them off and clean them one at a time. We got 10 cents a bushel for them, shelled out like oysters. They're beautiful to eat — lovely.

"I started swordfishin' in 1924. We'd go in 100-foot-long schooners with a crew of eight men. It was like whaling. Five men would go aloft on the topmasts. The man on the very top was called the mast headman. He would direct your vessel on to the fish once the others spotted a fin. The captain was most always the striker, the man who harpooned the fish from the pulpit of the boat.

"The harpoon is attached to an iron pike which turns the dart. Then the whole harpoon is hooked to a line which is attached to a half-barrel keg, tied to the boat by a 100-fathom line.

"Once a swordfish is harpooned, he'll go swimmin' off with the keg draggin' behind to mark and tire him. Some of these fish would sound out of

sight with the keg. You'd slip your painter through the strap of the keg and hang on to it. You never tied your painter to the dory — a swordfish could take you with him otherwise. If he sounds past 100 fathoms, you let go. That way you lose the fish, but not your life.

"When you're in a dory haulin' in a swordfish, you watch the line. If the strain suddenly slacks, you jump right up on the risings and straddle the boat. Men have been killed before by the fish's sword that rips right through the dory hull. If you're rammed, you're supposed to break the sword off and rip off parts of your shirt to calk the hole.

"The first time I went sword fishin', I was gone 31 days, 200 miles out on George's Bank sou'east by south of here. On that trip I caught the biggest fish of my life. He weighed 400 pounds. They averaged 200 pounds. We brought it into Portland and fetched about 10 cents a pound. Nowadays they get over $2 a pound.

"From 1934 to 1940 I ran sardines with Captain Holbrook. We used to find them by stamping the deck of our dory. If there was a school out there, they all splash out of the water as sudden as a ball of fire. Today they find them with mechanical soundin' machines.

"We'd catch sardines in nets 100 fathoms long. They had calk buoys strung all the way along to keep them afloat. We'd anchor all four corners of the net and set a purse seine inside it from another boat to close the bottom and haul in the catch. A seine is a net with a quarter-inch mesh that fish can't escape through. It stretched from three to 12 fathoms deep.

"Usually schools of fish hugged the shoreline, so we'd set our nets up ahead of them. We mostly caught herring and sardines in the pockets of the seine that way. Got from $10 to $12 a case for them. Now it's over $1 a can.

"I also used to go trawling. We'd be dropped off in 14 dories from the schooner, each with four tubs of trawl. There were 10 double shards to a tub. There's 50 hooks to a double shard, so about 500 hooks to a tub. Once the captain drops you off, you set sail downwind, and dropped your trawl until all four tubs of baited hooks were out behind. The dories would stay close together, and the captain would memorize where each was.

"When you hit bad weather, the captain signalled you back by lowering the jumbo sail inside the jib. You were supposed to cut your trawl, sink it down with weights, and mark it with a buoy. Then you'd wait to be picked up. If you disobeyed orders and didn't cut your trawl — and everyone around you did — you'd drift upwind of the other dories. The captain wouldn't know

where to find you. Captain Holbrook lost three men that way in fog and vapor. I had taken the place of one of those lost men.

"The worst fear at sea was of being run down by a steamer. In them days there was a pile of shippin' in the sea lanes from mailboats to passenger packetboats that ferried in from Portland. Quite a lot of fishermen got sunk in fog and at night. Often by the time you'd see one of those big ships, it was too late. They moved fast.

"If you still had time, you'd sound your horn. That didn't mean that you'd be heard. Then you'd either go right from them, or right for them; if you're sideways, you're a bigger target to hit.

"You know, Bailey Island has changed some since I first lived here. There was no bridge to Orr's Island until 1928. You'd have to row across, and then take a horse and buggy to Brunswick. We'd all go down to Steamboat Wharf four times a day to meet the Portland packets laden with groceries, supplies, and mail. In 1917 the whole bay froze over, and they couldn't get in. People were driving from Portland to Seguin in their automobiles. The harbor froze up like that again in 1934, but Coast Guard cutters were able to break it up.

"In the summer the tourists came. We had several grand hotels on the island, two dance halls, and an ice cream parlor. We'd have clam bakes, bean suppers, and events in the halls. It was grand back then."

STINSON DAVIS

Five Islands

STINSON DAVIS *is one of the last blue-water schooner captains who grew up before the mast, shipping granite and timber. Born in 1884, his needle-in-a-haystack memory has stored generations of detail. He recalls the routes and currents of six of the seven seas the way landlocked truckers remember the way home to Hoboken. He has shaken more sand and sea out of his boots than most of us ever will. He is a living anachronism.*

Cocooned in the musty parlor of a house in Five Islands, Davis surrounds himself with adventure books and cosmopolitan clutter. The walls are populated with photographs of schooners he mastered: the Maude Palmer, Henry Withington, Maria O. Teel, *and* Rebecca A. Taulane.

As the captain speaks, his fists clench, eyes flare, and his authoritative lower jaw thrusts. "We didn't know we was makin' history back then," he says. "For us, the schooner trade was just a routine job."

STINSON DAVIS / *Five Islands*

"I'M THE LAST OF THE BIG SCHOONER CAPTAINS. Was born right here near what is now Reid State Park. After grammar school I had no money, so I went to sea as an apprentice.

"I was 16 years old when I first shipped out on the *Sunbeam*, a local schooner carrying stones (granite) from Stonington to Boston for 50 cents a ton. I went on to carry stone from every damn hole in this coast.

"I worked my way through the various ranks, shippin' in the coal trade, the lumber trade, and the whale oil trade. After carryin' stones, I shipped out as second mate on the *Rebecca A. Taulane.* My brother, William, was captain of her. I was 18 years old, and was gettin' $35 a trip.

"I was shipwrecked on the *Taulane.* We were takin' a load of lumber from Jacksonville to New London in January. Off Cape Hatteras, she sprung a leak in a heavy gale. We worked the hand pumps for two days, but she filled up and then rolled over on her beam ends. My brother and I cut the masts out of her, and she came back onto her feet. We drifted around the North Atlantic, hangin' on in cold and ice on top of the cabin house. The lifeboat had been smashed off by seas mountains high. We were picked off by a steamer that took us to Cuba. From there, we returned to New York.

"At age 19, I was second mate on the *Maria O. Teel* from February to July of 1902. After I left her I shipped out as mate on a New Bedford schooner in the whale oil business until 1904. We'd go out to Dominica in the Caribbean to Prince Rupert Bay, a free port. The whalers used to make a full circle over six months, and congregated there. Crews on shore leave would spend their money there. We'd load up with oil, and bring it to New Bedford. That business was kind of stinky. From New Bedford we'd make a couple of lumber trips to the Azores — what we called the Western Islands — and then head down to Madeira and the Canary Islands to take on more whale oil which we'd ship to Cuba.

"I became master of the *Henry Withington* at $75 a month in 1906. By 1908, at age 24, I was captain of the *Maria O. Teel.* Wasn't too unusual. Boys often went to sea with their fathers who were captains. Their ways were often paved. But you could still work your way up in a short time. And I could take care of myself too. I weighed 175 pounds and was brought up tough. If there was any trouble with the crew, I had the law on my side — and a big .44 revolver.

"The only trouble I ever had was when a big black sailor from Virginia tried to take over the ship. He weighed about 200 pounds and told me what he was gonna do. I says, 'Are you all through?'

"And he says, 'No.'

"So I pull out my revolver and ask, 'Are you all through now?'

"And he says, 'Yes.'

'When we got to Jacksonville, Florida, he went right over the rail, and we never seen him again. Didn't even wait around to collect his money. The rest of the crew and officers stayed out of it. It was my fight, and they kept their mouths shut. So I let that fo'cas'le liar know who's boss. Never had trouble again, except with occasional rummies.

"After the *Maria O. Teel,* I went into the *Maude Palmer,* a four-master belonging to the Palmer fleet in Portland, Maine. We shipped out to Boston with a load of salt. Got into a hurricane, and she pretty near filled up on me. I got into San Juan, Puerto Rico, and the salt was partly dissolved. Of 3,000 tons, only 1,000 pounds were left, and there was 15 feet of water in the hold. I brought her back for repairs to Newport News in Virginia, and left her. A friend of mine took over her next, and I later learned that all hands were drowned in a hurricane. That were the end of the *Maude Palmer.*

"The *Maude Palmer* was the worst sailing vessel I was ever in. Steered bad. You could throw a cord of wood over her stern in Cape Cod, and she'd tow it in her wake all the way to Bangor. She was full aft, but the rudder didn't have much effect on her. She'd swing one way and then t'other. I had to steer somewheres in between.

"One time, just before Christmas, I came up from Norfolk in the *Maude* with a load of coal. Reachin' Nantucket, I anchored, waitin' for a chance to round the Cape. First thing I know there's this CRASH—BANG. When I jumped up and over the companionway there was all the riggin' and jib boom of a schooner layin' on my deck. The long boat was gone, and the wheel smashed off. We was hit, needless to say. A Nova Scotia schooner by the name of *Lady Smith* did it. Some lady.

"Well, the next day I got some canvas over our stern, nailed up the wheel, and took an extra boat down there to the vessel that hit us. That night, as I was layin' in bed, I soon heard some more yellin' and screechin' on deck. Again I rushed up and over the companionway, and here come another big schooner. The tide was runnin' off to the le'ward, so I got a megaphone and hollers, 'Keep off, Captain, you can't get by me.'

"He didn't even flinch, and his vessel hit us right in the fore riggin', tearin' off the lines. So he drifted off and anchored by the *Lady Smith.* We was all anchored side by side, lookin' an awful mess in the Slew of Nantucket Shoals, and that's how I was smashed up by two ships in one day.

" 'Course, since these two schooners run into me, they had to pay the damages. Next day a big cutter from Portland towed me back into Percy and

Small's shipyard in Bath for repairs. Put new masts in, a new stern on, and shipped my load of coal on up to Bangor. I never did have any luck with the *Maude.*

"Next, I was spare captain for New Haven, pilotin' vessels for sick captains. When World War I broke out I shipped out in the *William E. Downes.* Sailin' then was dangerous, but it was my job. If it was all calm and easy — why, all the women would go to sea.

"Durin' World War I we had to clear through customs before departin'. We got our papers, and wasn't allowed to say where we was going — we was just cleared for sea. They'd check our provisions. If you was over quota, they'd fine you. The customs people assumed you was goin' to meet a German U-boat at sea and ship her supplies.

"Them U-boats was thick. Why, a submarine sunk my brother's ship right off Barnegat Bay in New Jersey. Two days later I sailed through the wreckage comin' up from the Amazon and Buenos Aires in South America with a load of timber.

"My brother, William, was eight years older than me. He was sailin' the *Jacob M. Haskell,* a four-master. He was bound for New York from Norfolk, Virginia with a load of coal. They was eatin' dinner when the cook comes down and nervously says, 'Captain, there's a German submarine along side of us.'

"My brother went out on deck, and the captain of the sub calls out to him, 'We'll give ya five minutes to get off.'

"My brother calls back, 'Pretty short order, isn't it? Five minutes?'

"So the sub captain says he'll give him seven minutes. By the time my brother and his crew were in the yawl boat, the Germans were aboard the *Haskell,* placin' a time bomb on her. They didn't want to waste a torpedo. They took the oil from the engine room, the provisions, and then they sunk her.

"My brother and the crew made it to the Jersey beach when a storm come up. They had to hang onto the poles of a fishin' net all night until a steamer come along and picked them off. They went on to Martha's Vineyard, but were turned back 'cause another sub had just blown up the lightship. Finally they took off in the yawl boat, sailed through the Cape Cod canal through the blockade and into Boston Harbor.

"Toward the latter part of World War I, I was in the African trade on the *Matawoc.* We anchored off the Gold Coast in May, and never got away

until October waitin' for a load of timber. Food was all canned and salted horsemeat.

"You know the old poem about horsemeat? It goes:

'Old horse, old horse, what brought you here?
I've carted sailors' baggage for many a year,
From Sagarack to Portland pier,
Until killed by hard knocks and ill abuse,
They salted me down for sailors' use.'

"The salted horsemeat would preserve on long hot voyages. Got 300 pounds for $35. Now it costs over $1.25 a pound. Same meat.

"We also used to go fishin' to supplement our diet. We'd tie a rag on a hook and get down under the bowsprit on the dolphin striker. Then we'd lower a line and jig it. The snapper would bite, and you'd grab him. Sometimes a shark would come along and cut the fish loose. So we'd take an iron shackle, put it in the blacksmith's furnace, and heat it red hot. We'd wrap a piece of horseflesh around it and throw it overboard. The shark would grab it, and, oh boy, you see him go into a frenzy. Then the other sharks would go after him.

"In Africa we used to steer up the Congo, a damn big river some 3,000 miles long. We'd head for Banana Creek near Livingston's Falls where the water shoots through cliffs and then rushes 12 knots through the channel. Two parts of the Congo River are in rainy season all the time, so it's always boilin'.

"I wouldn't go past Banana — I wanted the Belgium Congo Bank to tow me so they'd be responsible for our cargo. Carried everything from cars to beer and missionary stores. When the Bank refused I said that I wouldn't budge. You see, if a hawser should break in the Congo, you're licked — you'd lose your ship. So we just sat there.

"Soon, I had the damn fever — malaria. I was so sick, I couldn't stand up. They used to shoot 40 grains of quinine into my bottom every day. I couldn't hear nothin', I couldn't see nothin', and all I could taste for months was quinine.

"Normally, to fight disease at sea, we had a medicine chest with some numbered bottles and a doctor's book. No doctor. If you could match the numbers of the bottles to the description of the ailment in the book, the sick man would get some medicine. Otherwise, we'd give him salt.

"Finally, I went ashore, met the Swiss in charge, and gave him a couple of quarts of Scotch whiskey. I wanted to get my manifest ashore and get out of there. Got him so well lubricated that he took responsibility for carting the cargo up-river himself.

"I shipped in the *Tolima* for seven years in the African mahogany trade. When that was over, most of the schooners was finished.

"By the end of World War I sometimes it would be four months or more before we'd get any news or mail. There were cables, but we couldn't depend on them in case the message were picked up by the enemy. Often we'd just hail the captains of passing vessels, and give them news by flags to take home with 'em.

"We used to go to South and Fulton Streets in New York City to round up a crew. Used a shippin' agent — didn't shanghai anyone in those days. The agent would charge me $1.50 per man, and sometimes could round them up in a couple of hours.

"We had a routine onboard ship. The day usually began around 7:30. The captain ate at a table with the first mate, and the second mate ate with the engineer. The eight sailors lived and ate in the fo'cas'le.

"As captain, I did the navigatin' along with the pilot. I generally took a sightin' of the sun with a sextant and a log at 8:00 in the morning. Got my longitude. At noon I'd sight the sun again for latitude and the correct time. Then brought your longitude back up to your latitude to get your position.

"To measure our speed and distance we used an old-fashioned log. The log was a triangle-shaped board with a rope through it. The rope had knots tied in it at intervals. The mate tossed it over the stern, and would sing out 'Time' everytime a knot in the rope passed over the railing. We measured the time with sand in an hourglass, brought in the log, and compared the time with the distance we travelled measured in knots. It took three men and a monkey to do that performance, but it was necessary.

"There were two four-hour watches. The captain's watch was the starboard one, and the mate's was the port one. There was also a dog watch to break up the monotony of the same schedule over a period of years.

"The watches was necessary. In them days the damned ocean was full of steamers and every other damn thing that floated. You wanted to avoid gettin' hit, especially durin' the war when we ran lightless to avoid being seen by U-boats.

"By the end of the watches it was time for dinner and bed. I never took my clothes off 'cause of the cold.

"This routine went on for years and years, but sometimes it was broken by strange things. We once ran into Saint Elmo's lights. We were before an eas'erly, it were raining, and the boy at the wheel cried, 'Captain, what's that?'

"I followed his fearful gaze and there on the mizzenmast is this electric glow. It lit up all the riggin' and was jumpin' from one mast to the next. Then it jumped clear off and leaped into the sea.

"I says to the boy, 'That's the devil, and he's come lookin' for ya.' Scared him good.

"Another time, I was struck by lightning. Two squalls were passin' each other and started a-twistin' like a cyclone. Started to suck up the sea in a water spout. Busted on us once, and dumped a devil of a lot of water.

"So I let the tops'ls run down and left the number four and five jibs runnin'. Then the foresail split. I stood by the spanker riggin' and told the mate to lower her when all of a sudden, I fell down flat.

"I got up, felt shaky, and wondered what the hell had just happened to me. Turns out that lightning had struck the iron rod on the topmast, and I had my hand on the rigging. It stunned me, and then grounded in the sea.

"I've fallen overboard before. One early morning, eas'ard of Cape Cod, I was fishin' when I slipped over. Thought I went down a mile, but heaven knows I barely wet my hat. I come up alongside the bowsprit chains and pushed my arm right in there.

"Now, I'd had a little trouble with rummies on this trip, and one of 'em seen me go overboard. He walked away calmly, and took his time before informin' the mate that the captain had just fallen overboard. The mate rushed over, threw me a rope, and hauled me in.

"I never could swim. One time a woman asked me how far I was from shore when one of my ships anchored, and then sunk to her anchors. I says, 'About a mile.' When she asked me why I didn't swim in, I told her, 'The mile was straight up and down.'

"The last vessel I had in the European trade was the *Tolima*. I was comin' back across the Atlantic in hurricane season, and Jesus, I run right into one. It was makin' the swing.

"What's it like in a hurricane? HELL. They swing 'round in a circle. In the middle is the eye — a windless vacuum. Everything inside is clean with a blue sky above. But you get in there, and the seas are piling up all around you on all sides of the compass. It's hard to tack right so you're comin' up to the waves. On the wrong tack you'll roll sideways into the trough of the seas, and it would pile to hell all over you. When that happened you had to rush to put your head plumb against the sides of the cabinhouse, or the waves would knock you and crack your head like an eggshell. It was safer up in the riggin' in a gale — less of a chance of gettin' washed overboard. But with snow and sleet, it was cold. Took up to eight hours sometimes just to reef in the sails with your bare hands. It's lots of fun.

"On the *Tolima* I had my wife and baby below in a room. We cushioned it with mattresses on the sides so that when she'd heave down, they'd survive. We were in that hurricane 24 hours. The mate went crazy, and two sailors turned sick. Pulled into Cape Breton where we put them into a hospital, mustered another crew, and brought her home.

"I retired back here in Maine at age 88. Nobody ever told me I had to get out, so I stayed on with a steamer license. I was brought up on schooners, stayed with 'em, and watched them all sink into watery graves."

WILLIAM SHEW

South Bristol

Boatbuilding can't be taught. It must be felt.

— WILL FROST

MAINE *harbors 2,400 miles of coastline, and about that many boatbuilders. People such as Vinal Beal, Harvey Gamage, and Will Frost. People for whom boatbuilding is a way of life, felt and breathed.*

Robert Pirsig understood this obsessive lifestyle. In Zen and the Art of Motorcycle Maintenance *he examines the ancient Greek concept of areté: virtue, excellence, quality. To be inspired with areté is to lose track of time, to blend work with life, to live with inner peace. Areté is that trinity of quality, mind, and matter that lives in fine crafts-manship.*

William "Dick" Shew lives in South Bristol. He wears comfortable wool sweaters, frayed at the elbows and neck. He looks quizzically through glasses that tend to slip from the bridge of his nose. He'll turn a phrase with the neighbors, tinker with his rusty John Deere tractor, and muck around the Cove in galoshes. All the while he is scheming up new racing shell designs.

Shew's alter ego is Cecil Burnham — a heavy, taciturn man who smiles through gapped teeth. He used to commute to work by rowing a peapod across Christmas Cove.

Shew's eighteenth-century saltwater farmhouse is a dowdy, mawkish piece of archi-

[3 9

*tecture hunkered down into the rocks. The boatshop is in the barn. Pallid winter
sunbeams filter through skylights, catching floating motes of dust and blue woodsmoke.
The walls are covered with exposed silver insulation. Booms hang haphazardly from the
rafters. Blueprints are tacked to supporting beams.*

*Shew and Burnham work in tandem on the boats, lofting, fitting, gluing, and
clamping. They stand back from their work like artists at an easel, chins cupped in hands,
elbows absent-mindedly suspended over heads. They judge lines and symmetry. Absorbed
in concentration, they are inspired with areté.*

Dick Shew / *South Bristol*

"I was interested in boatbuilding ever since age 12 when I made my
first. After completing Colby College I worked for Harvey Gamage here in
South Bristol, and Gaudy and Stevens in Boothbay. During that time I met
Cecil Burnham.

"In the 1960's neither Cecil nor I wanted to follow the trends and work
with fiberglass. We decided to stick with the 4,000-year-old tradition of
wooden boatbuilding and went into business for ourselves. We were just two
stubborn people who didn't like working with plastic.

"Fiberglass smells and is hazardous to your health. Beyond nine years a
fiberglass hull wouldn't hold up. The thermal-setting resin in the plastic continues to cure. Despite inhibitor chemicals it begins to chalk and crack. It
doesn't pay to fix it. You'll never see an antique fiberglass boat. They were
part of the planned obsolescence syndrome.

"On the other hand, there was something very life-like about working
with wood. Your boats have a backbone (keel), a rib cage (framing), and the
whole process is very personal. They vary from builder to builder — you put
your soul into them. They may not be as fast as the sleeker, fiberglass craft,
but you can replace rotten planking and keep them alive. And they do have a
life of their own. They come into the wind better than the fiberglass boats
on their own, for example.

"Somewhere along the line I was exposed to the old boats of the Her-
reshoffs, which were scattered all over New England. Nathaniel Herreshoff's
son, L. Francis, had his father's gift and feeling for making boats which were

beautiful and alive. Cecil and I visited him, and learned a lot. We returned with some of his blueprints. One of his boats is on the trestle of our shop right now.

"Boatbuilding was great, but we realized that we were living hand-to-mouth. It was a long time between pay days. To subsist I bought some rabbits which I bred out back for meat. We have a small vegetable garden and some pigs on eight and one half acres. In the late 1970's we bought three goats, intending to provide our own milk supply. We bred them and started a side business until the price of fuel forced us out in 1980.

"We learned that goats were fastidious eaters. If you put food down in front of them, they'll only eat it if it's clean and wholesome. They are naturally curious. Their mouth can feel things, so they're always testing stuff out. But the reputation of eating anything is a misinformed one.

"The goats are characters, especially the bucks. We named one 'Christmas Cove Messiah,' but we called him 'Messy' for short. The other was 'Shagbar Balder' — the Norse god of spring and flowers. He's flowery all right in an odious way.

"In fall and winter, during breeding season, it's every buck for himself. They have tremendous sex drive, stop eating, and worry themselves into spare condition. They have all kinds of fancy tricks like urinating on their beards. They'll bout, splutter, and blubber at each other and perform all sorts of humorous antics.

"Then we had the 'A.I. Kid' who was artificially inseminated. She's very curious — always looking through our windows to see what we're up to. And fantastically stubborn. When she didn't like something, the lower jaw would drop expressively. You could plan on having an uncooperative goat from that moment on.

"A.I.s daughter was 'Swayback.' She's an awful mouthy talker. She'll bellow and blubber. It's more than ordinary bleating. It's criticism.

"The wonder of the farm was 'Cupid.' She gave us close to 5,000 pounds of milk in 10 months. Upon hearing that, the milk inspector pointed out that even the best cows in Maine rarely equal that.

"The parallel between our two businesses revolved around energy conservation. We were pioneering a traditional subsistence lifestyle — something that I'd hate to see disappear in Maine. Both businesses are low-energy, low-overhead operations that could theoretically support a small community like South Bristol. Think of all the transportation and energy wasted to import boats and milk to Maine from California and the East Coast. What tremendous waste. Our little operation in South Bristol should be looked at as a future alternative as the price of oil soars with inflation. Still, people wouldn't change until they're put to the line.

"Although my lifestyle is very traditional, the conservative townspeople still think I'm a little funny. Ironically, they're a little skeptical. Still, you can be an individual here in Maine. I appreciate that above all else."

LANCE LEE

Rockport

Tradition is apprenticing, hands-on learning, natural

materials, wood, tools. It is dreams, and forging those dreams

into small watercraft. It is a discipline and way of life that

is five thousand years old. . . . Tradition is the Apprenticeshop.

— THE ONCE AND FUTURE APPRENTICESHOP

THE APPRENTICESHOP *existed in Bath under the aegis of the Maine Maritime Museum for 10 years. There, master craftsmen taught apprentices to build traditional wooden boats in a "labor-for-learning" experiment with no tuition or pay.*

The original Apprenticeshop was built in 1972 on the site of the old Sewall shipyard. It was constructed by apprentices in post-and-beam style with recycled timber and cedar shingles salvaged from a Waldoboro sail loft. It fit in with the nautical heritage of Bath: nineteenth-century sea captain houses with ornate decor, porthole windows, cupolas, and widow's walks; the Percy and Small boatyard; and the Bath Iron Works with its massive crane towering over all.

Since the 'Shop's opening its apprentices and interns have built traditional bateaux,

Grand Banks dories, Norwegian prams, a Soğnabat, Whitehalls, Isle au Haut skiffs, Phippsburg Hamptons, Quoddy workboats, Penobscot and Matinicus peapods, Herreshoff dingies, and a Tancook Whaler. The boats are sold to fishermen and to the public. The income helps keep the 'Shop afloat.

In 1982 the former Penobscot Boat Works on Sea Street in Rockport became the 'Shop's new site. There the traditions continue as boats are lofted, patterned, and molded into craft that would otherwise pass out of existence. In 1983 the 'Shop will finish another Maine Pinky which will be put into service in Penobscot Bay as a floating school for students interested in learning traditional fishing techniques.

Lance Lee started the Apprenticeshop in 1972, fulfilling an obsession to wed academic theory to a practical lifestyle. Surrounded by rolled-up blueprints of wooden boats and grant proposals, he sits with hands clasped behind his head and his Bean boots resting on the rim of a woodburning stove. Square-jawed with a jutting, opinionated chin, he leers rakishly beneath his red Norwegian toque.

"At the Apprenticeshop, we seek to collect the folklore of boatbuilding, to teach apprentices craft and style, and to publish our findings," he said. "We want to get this lore back in circulation."

LANCE LEE / *Rockport*

"IT took me a few years after graduating from Bowdoin to realize that some of the brightest people I've worked with and some of the most profound philosophers were the people who worked with their hands and who lived their beliefs rather than merely professed them. These individuals lived by their wits and common sense, and not from what they could buy. These individuals drew me closer to a working philosophy that is not simply pragmatic, but joyful and sustaining; sustaining of themselves in a spiritual fashion as well as of their families, their cheese and their bread. That's kind of exciting to me.

"There's a ritual way of living when your play and your work become synthesized. Little kids have no difficulty with this at all. A little kid will enter into the game of bringing in firewood because it's not only being helpful, but it's fun!

"Somewhere along the line, those kids grow up and change. Adults come to think that there is 'work' and there is 'play,' and you can't have them both at the same time. I don't believe that.

"It's a matter of using your hands as well as your head. Unfortunately, the intellectual community has come to consider using your hands to be a menial business and thinks that manual labor is a Portuguese fisherman. I've found that it's still possible to discover that manual labor can work up satisfaction as well as sweat, and something else besides. . . .

"I guess it's that 'something else besides' that I got interested in. It's hard to put a tag on it. An old boatbuilder named Charlie Blaisdell put it as well, I suspect, as it can possibly be put. In the last years of his life he said, 'Oh, we didn't have any money. No, nobody had any money. . . . People just lived different. They lived different!'

"I've been chasing down how to 'live different' without getting poverty-ridden or downtrodden. I'm beginning to suspect that one of those ways is to become so impassioned by what you're doing that you don't *resent* time or feel a desire to watch the clock and stop. When you're through with a day's work, you don't find diversions as needful. You don't push to get away from 'work' and begin 'play!' That's the ritual way of living, and it's what Charlie Blaisdell meant by 'living different.'

"In setting up the Apprenticeshop I had the Middle-Age precedent of apprenticeship in mind. Back then there were practitioners in the culture who knew the secrets of a trade and who developed attitudes towards work, care, the integrity of the product, and towards getting by. They knew when to zig instead of zag, and passed all of this along.

"Apprenticing is drawn from that really magnificent non-verbal tradition. You put a kid of 14 or 15 together with a master who has served a seven-year apprenticeship with a woodcarver, cabinetmaker, or shipbuilder, and something rubs off that becomes a permanent part of that young guy's act.

"When I was a kid in a boatbuilding community on an island in the Bahamas, the way kids entered into the trade was to grind a stone for the older men to sharpen their plane irons and knives on. I didn't really realize what was happening until years later. These kids were associating work and play, but they were also subtly just watching. In this way the kids learned at what angle to set a draw knife at. They didn't learn because somebody said, 'Now, at 18 degrees you're going to be about safe.' And they didn't have to go to a book to learn it. One day a man would be busy. He would toss Benny a tool and say, 'Go put an edge on that.' I'm pretty sure Benny

[4 9

looked around and thought, 'I've never done that before, but I think I know how.' And he'd go and do it.

"That's pretty exciting stuff because the mind isn't involved. The muscles become the memory bank, and something is passed along *naturally* rather than through words which intervene and disrupt sometimes as much as they serve.

"Words do serve, mind you. I'm not against words and recognize that there are skills involved in communicating and writing and in putting down a plan. I'm not an enemy of words and don't think anybody in our world should be. Words are tools, but I suggest that they've been dulled instead of sharpened!

"In learning to build traditional boats the Apprenticeshop has no tuition or wage. I believe in 'labor for learning,' and so the work that's done here on the boats, taking inventory, making tools, and running the place equals the apprentices' tuition.

"Even though we're affiliated with the Bath Marine Museum I would hate to see the Apprenticeshop perceived as simply belonging in a museum. It doesn't. It belongs, and is, in the marketplace which is a pretty good place to be. We're up against finances and real problems.

"We're not trying to make a statement about how good things were before, nor are we geared to the romance of craftsmanship. We're not trying to sustain the past for the sake of the past 'cause I don't give a rat's ass about the past for the sake of the past. What interests me is the quality of the future. What will keep that quality high are people who care about what they're doing, and who want the hand as well as the brain involved. This goes back to living your philosophy instead of just professing it.

"I'm interested in folklore and oral history, especially in the intricate old tricks of self-sufficiency that have plain straight left us or are on the wane. These tricks give a culture depth, like making stained glass windows, pattern-making, or inventing an apple peeler. These skills are disappearing from our world as the college placement bureaus continue to hold out only a certain spectrum of jobs. The really 'good' jobs are the highly professional lawyering, doctoring, and corporate heading. This is selling the society short as some of the manual skills are being lost and forgotten.

"These tricks were also passed down traditionally through the family. You don't find the skills in books or in class. And as family traditions are broken with our increased mobility, kids do something that their father and mother didn't do, and the chain gets busted. So it's through folklore and oral history that we should strive to get these skills back.

"My own interest in boatbuilding lore carried over from my family. After the Second World War my father's health was bad, and he had to be in a southern climate. So we moved from Cape Cod down to an island in the Bahamas which my grandfather lived on in the 1930's. My grandfather back then was greatly impressed with the Bahama people, and he liked the skills and extraordinary quality of their boatbuilding. Now, a good many years later, I am extraordinarily impressed with these islanders.

"One thing that impressed both me, my father, and my grandfather was the speed with which these islanders built their boats. My grandfather once placed an order for a 28-foot boat on a weekend. On Wednesday the island builders came to see him and asked if my grandfather would accompany them to the settlement to tell them if they were on the right track.

"When grandfather arrived he saw that they had already set up the transom, the stem, the stem apron, the keel, the two midship frames, and all of the ribbands! All the wood was hard native mahogany, and they had no electricity!

"How did they build so quickly? Those are the secrets that I'm spending as much time as I can trying to keep above the water. In many cases I know that they are just under the surface somewhere, and my effort is to raise them back up to a level of usefulness in somebody's life so the next generation can employ them.

"There are old tricks and skills on this Bahama island that have gone, but some of the oldest men there can still discourse about them. So I've returned to the island on occasion with a tape recorder to speak with them just as you're speaking with me. One of the things I'm hobbled by is that I don't really know the right questions to ask. I haven't built boats in their way, so it doesn't occur to me to ask certain things. Knowing how to ask questions for folklore becomes fragile as hell.

"To illustrate the importance of good questioning, let me tell you one of the most beautiful stories I know. A friend of mine named Keith MacArthur had the task of restoring a Massachusetts Humane Society lifeboat. He had the wit and intelligence to search all around until he found the coxswain of that particular lifeboat crew whose name was James Frost. Frost was very senior — I think in his 80's — but he was also very lucid.

"So Keith would sit down, and the old fella would just start to ruminate about the lifeboat. One day Keith mentioned that he found marks on both sides of the stern of an old lifeboat. He asked if the boat was steered with an oar as opposed to a rudder. Keith then wondered what the length of the oar was and if the boat was steered from the windward or the leeward side.

"The old fellow casually said, 'Well, she had *two* oars, of course. You had a tall man and a short man, and you had a short-oar and a long-oar.'

"Keith looked at him in astonishment. 'Short-oar?? Long-oar?? Oh! Then your long-oar was with the tall man, and your short-oar was with the short man, right?'

" 'Oh no,' replied Frost. 'The tall man had the short-oar, and the short man had the long-oar!'

"Keith found that this was a design for heavy seas. When you went over a wave in the lifeboat, the tall man with the short-oar could dig in by putting his oar deep in the water. And when they went over a long wave, the short man would crouch down, and his longer oar would rest in the wave which was 10 feet astern.

"Keith could never have reconstructed the lifeboat's steering system if it hadn't been for Frost, the old man. The accident of seeing the scars on the old boat, and then asking the right questions, did it.

"The next step is to put what you learn back into action, and that's much harder. Keith's Humane Society lifeboat was rebuilt in Mystic Seaport, and I hope they've tried her out in rough water to *prove* that you need a tall man and a short man to steer it!

"Another example of good questioning was when we started to build that Pinky you see there under the tarp. We sailed the *Vernon Langille*, a 35-foot Tancook Whaler that we launched in 1979, up the Kennebec to fetch the keel. We knew from speaking with Jim Stevens of Gaudy and Stevens in Boothbay that unseasoned red oak gets heavy and sinks. He told us beforehand to keep the oak tree that we felled for the keel afloat on a cradle of pine and spruce booms.

"We've put the *Langille* to good use over the years. In her first season she hauled 50 tons of cordwood to Monhegan Island. She's also transported sheep, granite, and cast-iron stoves. We collected a pile of local driftwood and sailed it down to Pier 16 in Manhattan. We sold the wood for $1,700 to some people who built an ale house out of it. And we've taken a crew of students from the Morse High School to help us sail a cargo of donated sardines and cordwood to Nantucket. We sold it and sailed to Plymouth where

we picked up a load of cranberries to ship back to Maine. Again, putting this kind of tradition and lore back into use is what the Apprenticeshop is all about.

"It's like a living parable for me to go back to this island in the Bahamas periodically. The perspective of returning again and again over the years since I was a kid has taught me a lot. It's exciting to study a culture that's 100 years behind us, or was until recently. They basically fish, farm, and build boats. But in terms of government and in terms of the skills of living, the culture was pretty advanced.

"Back in the 1940's the islanders lived in a form of very straightforward simplicity and didn't feel deprived of things. For instance, they didn't have refrigerators, but they always had fresh meat. How does that work?

"Well, it's a small island with a limited supply of pigs. So when you slaughtered a pig, you shared the pig out among your neighbors before it spoiled. And when the pig was all gone, somebody else slaughtered his pig. . . .

"But today on the same island, everybody has freezers. They no longer share. The poor have become very, very poor, and the rich have become very, very rich. Fences have been built up between the houses, and they get higher every year.

"There is something sad there. When the island was poor in the monetary sense, they were very strong in the communal sense. First, I saw the coming of electricity. Then came modern technology. Finally, tourists came, and with them greed and depersonalization. It is a living parable for me to see.

"Still, the more enormous the problem of depersonalization and the divorce of the hands from the head becomes, the more the countervailing forces have come out of the woodwork. Young people are coming to realize that small really is beautiful and that there is a saner and more resourceful way to live. And that's refreshing!"

PATSY HENNIN

Bath

Who knows but if men constructed their own dwelling with their

own hands, and provided food for themselves and their families simply

and honestly enough, the poetic faculty would universally sing when they

are so engaged. But alas, we do like cowbirds and cuckoos, which lay

their eggs in nests which other birds have built, and cheer no traveller

with their chattering and unmusical notes. Shall we forever resign the

pleasure of construction to the carpenter?

— Henry David Thoreau, *Walden*

A GEORGIAN BUILDING OF BRICK *rises five stories over Center and Water Streets in
Bath. For generations it was a furniture warehouse. A Masonic Temple, dubbed the
"Solar Lodge," graced its upper level.*

*In 1978 Pat and Patsy Hennin bought the dilapidated building for $40,000. They
moved in their four-year-old Shelter Institute, a housebuilding school. Once again, the
building houses craftsmen. In the Solar Lodge three solar panels heat water for the
bathrooms.*

Patsy Hennin keeps tools, plumbing pipes, and recipes in her eclectic office. Dressed in a folk skirt and blouse, she speaks with excited catches of airy breath. Her words cascade out in nervous spasms.

"We try to foster a can-do attitude in our students at Shelter," she says. "This attitude has never been foreign to Maine; people have never lost the link between providing their own food, clothing, and shelter. It's that old self-reliant lifestyle that we try to embrace."

PATSY HENNIN, / *Bath*

"PEOPLE who come to the Shelter Institute are those who usually yearn for an alternative to mass-produced society. They want to feel more responsible for their actions and environment. They don't want to be so dependent upon modern technology. They come from all over the world, and are all ages. As you can see from the pictures on the wall, the houses they build vary greatly in type and quality.

"At Shelter we use the house as our focus for teaching resourcefulness. The separation our society has made between cerebral activity and hand labor is disastrous. It starts at an early age in the public schools. Kids are tracked into college-preparation courses or industrial arts. One or the other. Whole generations have grown up with no faith or desire to try to fix plumbing or wiring. We call in experts: mechanics to fix the car, electricians to fix the lights, roofers to fix the leaks. It's terrible.

"It's ridiculous how housing had evolved. Today the trade is more for the ease of the builder than for the needs of the hirer. You see ticky-tacky builder's boxes all over the place, charmless houses that were erected cheaply to make the builder a quick buck. And they may have only learned one way to lay a foundation, and apply it everywhere no matter what type of soil there is beneath the house. As a result of their constrained thinking, people have cracked and leaky basements.

"This deterioration in quality and craftsmanship cuts across the whole spectrum from car mechanics to builders. It stems from a lack of caring. It has built an environment where life is out of most people's control. People come to Shelter to regain some measure of this control, to simplify their lives, and to learn to become slightly more self-reliant.

"People come to Shelter at an initial cost of $250 for 60 hours of technical courses. We start out with a three-week session where 100 people come to lectures on siting, foundations, framing, wiring, plumbing, insulation, and ventilation. That's in the morning. In the afternoon students go out and work as apprentices on houses being built in the area. They donate their labor free of charge. This helps the owners of the houses — everyone gains.

"People often sign up for our courses for economic reasons. The investment in knowledge yields a very quick financial return. By building a house yourself you can reduce the cost of a $100,000 house to $10,000.

"When I married Pat and moved from Long Island to Maine, we bought six acres of land in Woolwich. That was in 1974. We spent $5,000 to buy wood and building materials. Later we added a $2,000 addition, and a $3,000 barn. It was a devastatingly simply house. We slept with our two sons and our baby girl in a loft beneath exposed beams and framing members. The rest of the house was open indoors. It was heated entirely by wood, and there was an outhouse.

"We put that house on the market in 1982 and sold it in three days to a 35-year-old Bath Iron Works engineer. Our $10,000 investment sold for $52,000. Now we're building a more sophisticated house on 10 acres of shore frontage in Phippsburg. We've designed in a circular staircase of stone that leads up to a hot tub. We're living in a tent through the summer, and plan to have enough house to move into by fall.

"As with us, people building their own houses undergo a psychological change. Building a house forces you to confront yourself as you design your own living space. You become the poet staring at the blank page. You have to include your family and whole being in a design that's right for you. It's a personal thing, and very much a repressed desire in all of us. It is really exciting to give your children the gift of believing that they can build their own house and shape their own lives. Self-reliance becomes freedom."

WILLIAM

COPERTHWAITE

Bucks Harbor

MUDSEASON *arrives after a gruesome winter, and the road to Bucks Harbor winds rutted and potholed. Telephone poles heaved by frost tilt wildly from embankments, and the macadam undertread has cracked into a mosaic of decay. Past Cutler Harbor portions of the road have given up altogether and turned to mud. It will be a long time before they are repaved.*

Grizzled Mainers are profoundly unimpressed with spring. They are wary of false starts and lusty thaws. Still, hopeful signs well out of Maine's mud. Swallows build nests in rotten storm gutters and swoop between lightning rods on sagging barn roofs. Mourning doves coo at the rising sun from the telephone wires. Peepers croak and shrill in stagnant bogs. Trees sprout hues of peachblossom and lime.

During this season the road to Bucks Harbor is also in transition. Not content to merely deteriorate into mud, it narrows, bows, and vegetates. It bends and curves, pitches and yaws. It conspires, hoping to shrug off even the most determined, mapped-out motorists. Then, by a rusted truck mired in the ooze, the road ends. A thickety footpath leads through the spruce, opening into blueberry fields and clamflats. In the center of one of these fields are some oversized cupcakes containing one bald, grinning man.

William Coperthwaite is in a yurt, whittling a canoe paddle. He is austere with a compelling, sincere voice. He advocates a "new design for society," and he champions rural culture. As creator of the Yurt Foundation, he works to cultivate a resource bank for self-reliant living.

Yurts were originally goatskin huts used by Mongolian nomads. At Harvard University Coperthwaite adapted yurts to New England, creating practical wooden shelters that are inexpensive to build and mortgage-free. He built a yurt in the Radcliffe Yard and lived in it to prove his thesis. Since then, he continues to adapt folk knowledge to modern times.

WILLIAM COPERTHWAITE / *Bucks Harbor*

"WE live in an urban society dominated by urban values. Most of our art, drama, music, and media are centered in the cities. The term 'civilization' conjures up urbanity.

"I'm opposed to the idea that the city is the only place in which 'culture' and 'civilization' can thrive. We need to develop a philosophy of rural living to complement New York City with its sick theater/porno district, crime, and police. Now that we live in an age of telecommunications and TV, we can branch out of the cities. It's time to do so.

"We need to design better ways in which to live. I'm not interested in going back to the past and to the old ways, but in adapting culture from all time to the present. Right now we're in a yurt — a modern building. Although centuries old, they're still being designed right now. They're practical. I've blended Asian folk wisdom with modern science. Out of respect to the ancient nomads, I have kept the name 'yurt.'

"The yurt is a symbol of cultural blending. The Yurt Foundation seeks to collect and blend folk and scientific knowledge in all facets of life from agriculture to child care, housing, boatbuilding, family relations, and education. If we were all more conscious about how we thought our society should be, we'd have healthier, happier children and families. We'd be a healthier, more cooperative society.

"There is a lot of rebellion today. People say, 'We want to live simply and go back to nature.' Most of these people are well-intentioned, but they'll fail out there on their own. They don't have the know-how to really succeed. It's this kind of knowledge that I seek to collect.

"I have 250 acres of land here with no roads. I walk, ski, and snowshoe in, and that's delightful. I chose this site by the sea. Seafood and clams are a good automatic source of protein. I also pick blueberries, and garden. My aim is to remain as self-sufficient as possible, and to avoid grants. That way people can't say, 'You can afford to chop wood, dig clams, and tend a garden because of donations coming in from outside sources.' If I can't live simply I'm in no position to teach others how to do so.

"When I talk about simple living, I don't mean simple-minded living. I have nothing against industry or technology, but rather advocate a more selective use of technology. Like learning to make toys for your own children instead of relying on prefabricated plastic tank models that you buy in the store. I don't want to be deprived of the pleasure of making things for myself and for others.

"One of the sad things about our society is how we prostitute ourselves. We sell our brains, talents, and energy for money. Too many of us spend our lives working at jobs we despise. We look at the clock and hope for weekends and vacations. We get our kids in the same mold, teaching them boring material, and holding out grades.

"To a larger extent people ought to try harder to do what they like. The greatest barrier is thinking consciously or subconsciously that one can't find work that is enjoyable. The cost is huge in frustration, mental illness, crime, and unhappiness.

"People also talk a lot about conserving energy, but they're wasting it every day. Like joggers. You can get the same amount of exercise from chopping wood, and get double-value for your time and effort. The wood heats you twice − first in the cutting, then in the burning. It's all a question of values and of consciously taking steps to design a better society."

HUSTON DODGE

Damariscotta

If a man does not keep pace with his companions, perhaps it is because

he hears a different drummer. Let him step to the music which he hears,

however measured or far away.

— HENRY DAVID THOREAU, *Walden*

JOEL HUSTON DODGE *stands in an unheated woodshed, working on the dovetailing of a pine apothecary chest. He is long-legged and shallow-chested. His rounded shoulders are huddled against the cold as he breathes out vapor that steams his wire-rimmed spectacles.*

Dodge is eccentric from stem to stern. His undersized tweed jacket looks like it was liberated from some shabby yard sale. Indeed, it was. His wrists protrude obtrusively from frayed sleeves. Wool rag socks migrate up his legs, disappearing into worn corduroy knickers. His sombrero is oversized. The leather of his moccasins looks parched like the mummified remains of some lesser Pharaoh. The tips of the shoes curl at the toes, and inside cardboard is stuffed to cover the holes. Dodge may be a millionaire.

The old cabinetmaker believes himself reincarnated from ancient Egyptian masons. Frowning, he says that there are three important things in life, "Good health. Good friends. And brushing every morning to keep good teeth." Without batting an eyelash he removes his teeth, produces a frayed toothbrush out of a coat pocket, and goes to work.

Dodge has created a special world for himself. His front yard is garish, his back-

yard a bazaar. He has a slothful passion for wooden bric-a-brac and has scoured the countryside looking for old bones to add to his 27-acre mausoleum. Since his introduction to woodworking decades ago, no dump or dilapidated barn has been safe from the canny inspection of Huston Dodge.

In place of laundry, Dodge's mawkish clutter is stacked along linen lines as high as hands can reach and eyes can see. His world embraces the wrecks of birch bark canoes, broken broom sticks, warped ship planking, weathered clapboards, rusty bathtubs with splayed feet, refrigerators, old car and tractor graveyards, and small wooden stairways that ascend abruptly toward heaven. Narrow aisles drift through the maze, leading from woodsheds and creating unlikely crannies and nooks. A wormwood fence encloses the grounds.

The clutter continues inside the house Dodge built, a colonial-style saltbox composited from several ancient manses. Furniture is stacked along the walls. Dust and cobwebs hide magnificent pine paneling, ornate pilasters, corner cupboards, and a formidable mantelpiece. He heats his bedroom with a woodstove and sleeps on a mattress on the bare floor. Sunlight illumines dark recesses filled with jars of peanut butter, sunflower seeds, and canned tomatoes. He keeps no television, radio, or telephone.

In front of Dodge's house is an old army jeep covered by an olive tarp that is ripped at the seams. He hates to drive. When forced out by necessity, neighbors stare in disbelief. Dodge drives in the middle of the road, slowly, white knuckles clutching the steering wheel, shoulders hunched, eyes straining. People amble out of the way.

There is a method to the madness of Huston Dodge. He grew up among master cabinetmakers and shipwrights. Inspired by eighteenth-century furniture, tools, and skill, he attended trade schools and collected antiques. He developed a genius for fashioning replicas of eighteenth-century hutches, divans, rolltop secretaries, corner cupboards, and houses. This explains his clap-trap world — "You never know what may come in handy." And gives a clue to the beat of Huston's drummer.

H U S T O N   D O D G E / *Damariscotta*

"I started workin' at carpentry when I was 10 years old and carried through with that theme all my life. I was always interested in early architecture and building construction, like the barn workshop we're standin' in.

"I got to learnin' how to use old tools, especially chisels and planes. The old-timer shipwrights and cabinetmakers would show me like Ed Bates, a retired railroad engineer. He had a big long-handled mustache and was kind of gruff, but he taught me how to make wooden nails and how to use tools. I hung around him as much as I could. I also talked with Gus Jones and Charles Perkins who were old carpenters, and Jonah Moss and Hiram Bisby who built ships. Bisby was kind of disagreeable, but he taught me to frame buildings, how to figure out the length of roof rafters, and how to erect houses so they was plumb. I apprenticed for Hiram. He got upset with me 'cause I was interested in eighteenth-century work. He couldn't see what it had to do with the more modern work he was doin'.

"I used to build stage scenery when I was in school in the Wentworth Institute in Boston around 1939. I apprenticed with a blacksmith and learned how to weld hardware like iron and brass furniture handles. I get some of this material from the bathtubs and stuff I rescue from dumps. You'd be surprised what people throw away.

"To get practice I built wooden ship models and worked on projects. Like this eighteenth-century style drawer. I dovetailed the joints and made it out of Ponderosa pine and Douglas fir. It's the nearest thing to an old apothecary chest. I also built a lifesize playhouse out back between the ages of 10 and 21. I fashioned all the moldings and panelled the walls inside usin' materials from old buildings that I took down around the countryside. Some of the pilasters and trim in my house are from these dilapidated buildings too.

"I renovated an old grist mill out back by myself. Used gin poles and a come-along. I had to tear down seven buildings to build that one mill: two barns, one warehouse, three cottages, and one house. I built it using all the old tools and methods, lifting and fitting everything myself.

"I'm going to use that mill to run a lathe someday. I figure I can get 30 horsepower from the stream. All I have left to do is build the waterwheel. I

also hope to put a saw in the mill so I can cut and cure my own wood.

"Another project I did was to build a wooden pyramid. I keep it in the rafters of the mill. It's an experiment. I'm told that if you build a pyramid to the scale of the Great Pyramid of Giza and orient it true north, like mine, you can preserve food and sharpen razors under it. I've tried this. I suppose it works. The Ancients knew so much that we have forgotten. Much of this metaphysical knowledge was destroyed with the burning of the library of Serapis in Cairo during the third century A.D.

"During World War II, I was sent overseas to serve in England. I found all kinds of early things there datin' back to Celtic times. I used the War as an opportunity to study the construction of Norman churches, castles, and Gothic cathedrals. I found all kinds of antiques that I bought at a good price and shipped home. That's how I got into the antique business for a while.

"When I got back to the States in 1945, I tore down some more houses. Then I built the house I live in now. It's a composite of two eighteenth-century houses. From 1948 until 1976, I tore down barns and assembled a lot of the material you see here to put up more buildings. You never know what may come in handy. People throw away a lot of stuff thoughtlessly, from antique brass hinges to food in the backs of restaurants and old clothes. They don't understand why I salvage it.

"I once had a big hassle with the selectmen of this town. They called my place a 'junkyard.' They thought I was a hippie, and maybe I was. People were suspicious of my long hair and beard. They felt my place devalued those nearby. People are just paranoid of anything that's different. I put up a fence around the place so you couldn't see it from the road.

"Maybe I am a little different from most people, but to me, my lifestyle makes sense. I don't heat my house much 'cause I like to stay used to the weather. It's healthier. I dress different when it gets cold. Right now I have on about five thicknesses of clothes: two pants, two sweaters, two pairs of stock-ings, my hat, and this jacket that I found in a dump. Some people threw it away. Can you imagine? I also like to wear hippie beads. I've been going out to the deserts of California in the really cold weather since 1958 to hunt agate, petrified wood, and trace gold with friends. I live out of an old trailer and have, on occasion, slept in abandoned mine holes or wherever I happen to be.

"I like to stay healthy. I eat mostly vegetarian foods like nuts, peanut butter, dark bread, dried fruit, and powdered milk. You can find an awful lot of good food layin' around goin' to waste. People discard it in the backs of stores and restaurants. People waste so much.

"Anyway, I love carpentry. Carpentry is a process of trial and error. I had to teach myself algebra, trigonometry, and plane geometry in order to build houses. I think a lot of what I learned was reincarnated. I've gotten like the eighteenth-century cabinetmakers. After much practice, the symmetry and proportions of furniture is in my head. Back in the old days, you'd go to a fine cabinetmaker and tell him what you wanted. They'd think about it, and then design it. I can do that now.

"The eighteenth-century manner of construction had character. Character is when you build a reproduction by hand, and it looks the way it's supposed to look when you're through. It has the proper hardware on it and tenon joints held together by wooden pins like the originals. All of the surfaces should be planed by hand including the surfaces inside the drawer that you don't normally see. That gives a piece character and quality. It may have little imperfections on it like a tool mark. That's good — that's the way it's supposed to be. It isn't the same as some machine-planed mass-produced item.

"Character is also the knowledge that goes behind a piece of furniture. In the eighteenth century, there was country work and fine cabinet work. They was different. And in certain periods particular woods were used by tradition. The Queen Anne period used walnut as did the William and Mary period. The Pilgrims used oak. The Empire and Regency periods used mahogany veneer as well as the Chippendale and Hepplewhite periods. The Victorians used walnut and oak, although in this country they settled for curly ash, mahogany, birch, cherry, and even maple as a secondary unfinished wood.

"The differences between a work of art and an antique is the theory behind the design. Eighteenth-century furniture was art. It was built by craftsmen who cared, and who really knew what they were doing. It had character.

"Character is a very human instinct. It's like learning a language. You need a whole theory and conception in your mind to speak the language. You may even visit the country and people where the language is spoken. Once you do that, words fit in place and can be used eloquently. That's character."

HARRY SANDERS III

Greenville

D.T. SANDERS & SONS *was organized in 1848 by David Tildon Sanders. It has been outfitting sports and hunters in Greenville longer than many states have existed in the Union. Nestled in the north woods at the foot of Moosehead Lake, the store is a jumping-off place for people bound into the Allagash wilderness.*

D.T. Sanders & Sons was truly a "general store." It has served Greenville as post office, bank, grocery, haberdashery, ammunition depot, stables, town hall, and guide service. Like a magnet, it drew gossip through its simple doors. As one customer said, "The grapevine starts here."

Harry Sanders III perpetuates the dynasty. He stands behind the counter greeting customers by name. D.T. peers down from a dreary Victorian portrait. Next to him, the head of a full-racked bull moose sneers. Sanders senses the great responsibility hanging over his head. He gulps hard, bobbing his Adam's apple, and scratches the back of his head with hairy knuckles. Like royalty, he must someday decide to whom title of the store will pass.

HARRY SANDERS / *Greenville*

"I WAS BORN IN 1923 and am the latest son to own and manage D.T. Sanders & Sons. Before me was Harry Sanders I, my father; Harry Sanders Sr., my grandfather; and David Tildon himself, my great-grandfather.

[7 5

"Young D.T. was quite a worker. He was bound out to apprentice under M.G. Shaw in 1857 and was working like a wire of nervous energy, seven days a week in the store he later took over. That was the year Henry Thoreau came by here to get a guide and outfitted for a canoe trip into the North Woods. He based *The Maine Woods* on that trip.

"D.T. was only five foot nine inches tall and weighed 140 pounds, but he was exceptionally strong and savvy. He grew a beard. A customer once came in here and asked me if I believed in reincarnation. He was lookin' from the floor up to D.T.'s portrait on the wall. I looked down, and sure enough, there was this schnauzer with a beard just like D.T.'s.

"Greenville was definitely a frontier town back in the 1880's during D.T.'s heyday. There was nothing but forests, streams, mountains, and lakes to the north of us. The Bangor and Aroostook Railroad was just being built. It stopped here at Greenville Junction and tied into the Canadian Pacific line. The railroad crews consisted of cheap Chinese labor and Irishmen — a rough crowd. They laid tracks through the swamps all day. Then there were lumberjacks from the Old Country of Poland and Finland.

"When the 1880's financial panic hit, logging companies like Great Northern used to issue scrip in place of money. That held the logging crews around long enough for them to complete the drives down the West Branch Penobscot, Moosehead Lake, and into the Kennebec. The scrip was dated — it could only be cashed in on the day after the drive was completed.

"D.T. and my grandfather used to meet these loggers at night when they came into the pier. They'd get out the 'big black pocketbook', set a lantern out on a barrel, and they'd buy up the logger's scrip giving them so much on the dollar. That enabled the loggers to go off on benders in town, and D.T. to cash in the scrip and make a profit. It wasn't illegal, but it did make life difficult for the logging companies who had to sober the men up enough to get the drives completed. 'Course, the logging companies never said anything since D.T. Sanders & Sons was their lifeline supply of food and wangan (blankets, clothes, and tobacco).

"When these lumberjacks went on benders, they was a fightin' bunch. There was three places back then in the whole Union that was the worst places to be: the White River Junction House in Vermont; the Silver Dollar in Galveston, Texas; and the Push and Pull Saloon here in Greenville. They were wide-open towns — no law whatsoever. My father told me that hardly a night went by that somebody wasn't killed or hit over the head for his poke.

The Push and Pull used to be where the Long Branch Bar and Moosehead Hotel is today.

"Greenville was famous for being the start of Allagash River canoe trips. Guides like Black Hawk Farmer met sports right here down by the docks in front of the store. There must have been some 200 Indian guides in the Kineo Mountain area who came in here lookin' to get hired by city slickers. D.T. Sanders & Sons has outfitted everyone from Thoreau to Sir Harry Oakes and Chief Justice William Douglas. Even get the L.L. Bean Company people in here once in a while for Saint John River passes.

"We'd outfit sports from head to toe. We'd stoke their grub here in the middle of the floor, get them a canoe, a guide, map out their trip, put them in the lake, and then pull them out when they got back. We did that right up until around 1963 when people started bringing all of their gear along with them.

"I still have a list of all of the guides in the area, like that French Canadian gent standing over there. My family has used him for many years. If I speak French to him in front of other people, he'll ignore me. But if we're alone, he'll answer back in French. He used to take us from Greenville to Northeast Carry at the northern end of Moosehead Lake 40 miles away. From there, our gear was portaged by a team of horses to the West Branch of the Penobscot River which led us into Umbazooksus Meadows, Chesuncook, Mud Pond, Chamberlain Lake, Eagle Lake, Churchill Lake, the Allagash River, and finally up to the Saint John River almost 150 miles away. My father took that trip for 20 years. He had a camp on Chamberlain Lake and used to move his gear there on an abandoned flatcar, poling it up the tracks.

"Over the years the store has sold everything from clothes to cars and wagons, horses, and groceries. We even had a herd of cows out back once and sold their milk. We had a cracker barrel and a pickle barrel next to a big pot-bellied stove that canted out over the middle of the floor. At night D.T. and my grandfather would go over the books by a kerosene lantern. Old-timers like Dave 'Couchée' Coyote, a French Canadian who used to tend the horses in the stables here, would come in, light up their pipes, and exchange yip yap and hunting yarns.

"D.T. Sanders & Sons used to ship supplies up to the lumber camps by boat in fall and summer, and by horse-drawn tote teams in winter before Great Northern's 'Golden Road' was built. We'd steam up Moosehead Lake to Lily Bay and Kokadjo, Grant Farm, and Chesuncook. These places were all stopovers for the paymaster, company officials, and for tote team drivers. They had hay bins and stables, and fresh teams of horses waiting for you.

"I remember visiting one of these old logging camps with a manager of Atlas Plywood. We got there and entered a big log cabin dining room. The cook had set places for everyone at long tables, and everybody started eating like there was no tomorrow.

"A lumberjack's breakfast was beans, hams, steak, and fish. They took out big thick sandwiches and coffee on sleds into the woods for lunch. At dinner it was traditional beans, hams, steak, and fish again.

"I sat down to a table laden with beans, piles of mashed potatoes, hunks of cabbage, five different pies, donuts, and cookies as big as the pie plates. I saw all this food and started chirping.

"Well, I hadn't noticed how quiet everyone was, except for the sounds of eating, and a big bull cook runs over to me. He took a great big spoon and rapped it loudly on the table in front of me and boomed in a sonorous voice, 'YOU SHUT UP!'

"I was dumbfounded and couldn't eat another bite, but everyone started laughing. I was so embarrassed. No one had told me that it's a rule to eat in silence in the camps. With so many men to feed three times a day, if everyone talked the overworked cooks would never get any sleep. It was a matter of getting in and out quickly. I guess I was set up for that one."

LEON GORMAN

Freeport

ONCE UPON A TIME *Freeport was a sleepy little town just past the Eagle Motel and a 60-foot-high Indian statue on Route 1. Town was comprised of a drug store with a soda fountain, the historical society, a fish market, a variety-news store, and a barbershop. Saltwater farms lined the frost-heaved road to Wolf Neck. During harvest, bedrolled stacks of hay dotted uneven hillocks. Fog often rolled into town from Casco Bay, blurring Main Street. Every once in a while the sound of tires on wet pavement came through rain-stained windows.*

At night Freeport quieted down — just some moths circling desolate streetlights, the buzzing of electric generators in the Portland Clam Company, and a few feral cats and raccoons rummaging in the trash cans.

There was one other thing in town — the L.L. Bean Company. It was quiet too. Then the recreation movement hit, lowering on Freeport like a boom. Soon there were more streetlights for the moths, more electric generators, and when it rained, hundreds of tires on the wet pavement made Main Street sound like a rushing waterfall.

When the Freeport post office was inundated with Bean mail orders, the company received its own zip code. Open 24 hours a day, Bean's also took in the town fire alarm, paid plenty of town taxes, and sponsored town fishing derbies. As more people stopped by, Dansk moved in along with factory outlet stores to take advantage of Bean's tourist traffic. Soon Freeport was humming with activity.

The L.L. Bean Company has mystique. From moonlighting as a Bean salesclerk, I know that even in the single-digit hours of early morning the company is busy attending to insomniacs, Bowdoin students, hunters, fishermen, tourists, and truckers. The recep-

[8 1

tionists downstairs rarely stop answering the telephones. The ubiquitous cash registers never stop clicking.

Sure, Bean's is the only distraction in town past midnight (aside from the blinking stoplight on Main Street). But it's more than that. It's the thrill of personal discovery off Route 95. It's the idea that the place hasn't closed down in years except for a brief interlude one winter when the doors were blocked so wet snow could be shoveled off the roof. It's the memory of deer carcasses being weighed at the front entrance, the company game dinners, and Bean employee outings to cheer the Boston Red Sox. It's the creaking stair- cases, the green carpeting, and pine-panelled walls that seem to shift as the store expands every other time you visit. It's Fred Bean's moose trophy above the stairwell, and the tents set up downstairs. It's the clerks who mediate, suggesting to customers that they not *buy a certain item because they've tried it in the woods and found it wanting. It's no sign of recession for hundreds of feet in all directions. It's the great Amer- ican success story.*

Leon Gorman is the grandson of Leon Leonwood Bean. He speaks with quiet confidence. No surprise there; he is president of the company. L.L. Bean Company has grown from one million dollars of net revenue in 1937 to $3.5 million when L.L. died in 1967. In 1982 net revenues reached $232 million.

Leon Gorman is a generous man with sound business judgement. Although more introverted than his gregarious grandfather, Gorman has inherited L.L.'s reliable conservatism and practicality.

Gorman's office adjoins a vast warehouse on Casco Street. Inside are thousands of square feet of echoey ambiance. Forklifts run through the aisles, overshadowed by an inventory that includes chamois shirts, Mackinaw coats, guide jackets, Moose River hats, Hudson's Bay point blankets, herringbone twill tweeds, khaki trousers, and hunting shoes. Workers consult a computer to find the locations of merchandise. Semitrailers, poised for loading, back up to gaping bay doors. Bean goods are shipped to the far reaches of the world, all from Freeport — a town that harbors a company destined to live happily ever after.

LEON GORMAN / *Freeport*

"LEON LEONWOOD BEAN, my grandfather, was born in 1872 in Bethel, Maine and orphaned at the age of 13. He moved to Freeport around 1900 and became a partner with one of his brothers in a haberdashery. Still, ever since living on a farm, his lifetime interest was hunting and fishing which he did at every opportunity.

"In 1910, as legend goes, L.L. finally got tired of coming back from his hunting trips with nothing but cold, wet, sore, tired feet. He decided he'd develop a boot that would keep them dry. At the same time he wanted it to be light in weight and give him the support that normal rubber boots didn't offer. He set out with some old overshoes and just cut the tops off them. He sewed them back onto rubber boots creating the first topsiders.

"L.L. had a lot of enthusiasm, especially when things were combined with his interest in the outdoors, so he decided to go into the boot business. He found a local cobbler to cut and sew the leather tops to the rubber boots, and then he got a list of Maine hunting license holders. He began mailing out a brochure about his boot which he called the 'Maine hunting shoe.'

"L.L. started off with this 100 percent guarantee of complete satisfaction. Well, his first 90 pairs of boots out of 100 came back. He guaranteed them all, and fixed the leaks with the help of the United States Rubber Company (UniRoyal) in Boston.

"Despite a lack of formal education, he had a natural gift for writing copy. Never a modest person, he had sublime confidence in himself. His voice boomed, and he had a gregarious personality. He was impatient and couldn't stand to see us grandchildren knock a trout off a hook.

"All of this enthusiasm projected through his writing in mail-order brochures, making up for his lack of formal education. He personalized all of his products. He'd say, referring to his chamois shirt, 'This is the shirt I personally wear on all my hunting and fishing trips.' In another old catalog he plugged an assortment of trout flies, 'If you haven't caught any fish after using each of these six trout fly patterns, then you might as well go home 'cause the fish just aren't rising.' Those sort of things coming straight from the heart made him believable in a time of mail frauds.

"He moved across the street into the site of the present store, and went out of the haberdashery business altogether in 1917. He took space on the second floor of a building that enclosed a theater, barbershop, post office, printing press, and a variety store. His factory and showroom were all connected. Customers could wander all over the place. The stairways went through cutting rooms and offices, shipping departments and accounting areas. None of the floors really matched up. As the company grew additions were added, and the ramble of the store developed character.

"In 1920 L.L. added fishing tackle and camping gear to his catalog, and went into a wider selection of footwear and outdoor apparel. And in the 1930's he put a bell on the outside of the factory door. Anyone that wanted to find anything after-hours would ring that bell, and the night watchman would open the door and conduct the sale. At some point that developed into just leaving the door open all the time — the start of our being open 24 hours a day, every day of the year.

"Right from the start, L.L. was distributing by mail out of state. He was an early advertiser in *Outdoor Life* magazine and *Field and Stream*. This advertising created an increased demand for catalogs. As a result of this today's company does most of its business by mail order. We serve 50 states and ship to 70 foreign countries. Pound for pound, our best state is Alaska — 25 percent of the households in Fairbanks and Anchorage have our catalog. Maine and the snowbelt states are also strong. And overseas we do a good business with Japan. When I travel I look at people's feet. It's nice to see our company represented.

"In the 1950's and 1960's prior to the 1965 back-to-nature recreation boom, the company was tired and demoralized. It was going nowhere in a hurry. The product line was becoming obsolete, and its employees were nice, local, elderly people. The store was marginally profitable, and L.L. was getting on in years, 'content to get his three meals a day, and he couldn't eat four.'

"I just happened to luck into a situation. I had graduated from Bowdoin in 1956 and was in the Navy until 1960. I went over to L.L. and asked him for a job. He let me fill my father's vacant desk, buying apparel, and I began to learn about the business. I never anticipated that I'd become president. Had I known just how badly things were at the time, I might have picked up and moved somewhere else.

"Then in 1965 things started to move off center. The nation started returning to old-time values and interest in the outdoors picked up. Well, we

sure were an old-time value, and found ourselves well-positioned. We up-dated our product line and fine-tuned our advertising and catalog. . . .

"When L.L. died at age 94 in 1967, he had made a profound impact on the lives of Americans. He was written up in *Time,* and the *Huntley-Brinkley Show* gave him 10 minutes of air time. We got 50,000 letters as a result of that. And from there, things really took off."

RANSOM KELLEY

Bowdoinham

IT *is an orange-tinted mallard day in October, and Ransom Kelley's Labrador retrievers whine with anticipation from the back of the pickup. Nearing the reedy marshes of Merrymeeting Bay, they smell water. Kelley shifts the truck into third gear and barrels over a culvert at 30 miles per hour. The dogs are heaved into the air in a scrambling blur of hair, claws, and teeth. Desperately they try to maintain equilibrium with the bouncing metallic platform below. At the water's edge the wild-eyed dogs are positively frantic. They gulp air through smiling jowls, hearts thumping, webbed feet anxious to carry them through the water in search of ducks.*

Ransom Kelley fills out every inch of his rumpled clothes. A white beard curls around his chin, and his blue eyes are penetrating and patient. An able guide with a bottomless cache of yarns, he can hunt, trap, fish, and jack-all-trades. Most at home on the derelict back roads of his Bowdoinham farm, he takes pleasure in simple things: the slant of sunbeams, the smell of pine resin, the stonewall flitting of chipmunks — and duck hunting.

RANSOM KELLEY / *Bowdoinham*

"I am a Maine guide. I started guiding in the 1930's. Got my license after I proved that I could handle a canoe in white water, read a map and compass, and handle sports in the woods. I often took people into fishing camps on Moosehead and Rangeley Lakes.

"It was the guide's job to prevent sports from getting lost, and to cut the firewood, build campfires, and cook. We ate well. I'd rig a baking reflector to make biscuits and coffee, skinned out trout we caught, and packed in beer and an occasional steak. The guide had to look after sports as if they were babes in the woods. And he had to do so without their noticing. At night before bed, we'd swap yarns. In return the sports paid for your wages, food, and supplies.

"The original Maine guides were the Indians. They found their way around the woods by instinct, and could sniff out thousands of subtle signs from living outdoors all their lives. You get to feel these signs after a while.

"You listen to birds early in the morning. If a storm is coming, they're actively getting food in to their nests before it breaks. If you're out fishing, you open your catch up. If you find lots of gravel in, say, cod — get the hell ashore. They eat gravel before storms to take on ballast. You watch the sun when it rises and the color formations of the sky and clouds. You keep a track of wind directions and shifts, and look at the sun again when it sets. You read the stars at night for directions. You study topographical maps, and learn routes along streams and logging trails. You learn to dead reckon with a compass to get your directions. You can find north by seeing where the most moss grows on the sides of trees. All of this gets to be second nature to you.

"I've seen some pretty strange sights in the woods. One night I was walking through a deer stand. I kicked a few rotten logs and saw something glowin' green. Will-o'-the wisp. Apparently some kind of chemical action had started. I got to one spot, and there were these eight miniature street lights glowing green with phosphorescence on the ground. It was uncanny.

"At my farm on Abbagadasset Point, we overlook Merrymeeting Bay. The Bay is at the confluence of six rivers including the Cathance, Kennebec, Abbagadasset, and Androscoggin. It is wonderful breeding ground for ducks and Canada geese. It also attracts some hellish thunder storms. One storm will make its way down the Androscoggin River, and another will come off the Kennebec. They meet in the Bay and have one hell of a time circling 'round.

"I was feeding my cows in the barn when one of these storms hit. The thunder was tremendously loud, and I stood back from the barn door to avoid getting struck by lightning. All of a sudden this big ball of Saint Elmo's fire comes down. It passed between the house and the barn, and then tumbled

out into the Bay. Damnedest stuff you ever saw. It was about eight feet in diameter and burned with a cool blue light. It was weird."

"Erle Browne, my father-in-law, was one of the great Maine guides. He received his name from my wife's grandfather who was a drummer boy in the Civil War. During one of the battles he took a book out of a dead Confederate soldier's pocket. The hero of this book was named Erle Browne, and that's what he named his only son.

"Erle was very close to nature. He started duck hunting on Merrymeeting Bay when he was 13 and didn't quit until three years before his death at age 84.

"Over the years guides have worked to design better 'sneak boats,' otherwise known as scull boats or floats. These boats were low, round-bottomed skiffs. A hole in the transom just above waterline allowed you to insert an oar which you'd scull by turning and twisting with your arms and wrists. That propelled the boat forward without creating any turbulence that might disturb the ducks or geese.

"Erle and I decided to design our own Merrymeeting Bay sneak boat. We went out one night on a moonlight requisition for some wood, and created a boat that would blow right off straight no matter what quarter the wind hit it from. I've had excellent success in getting to geese with this boat.

"The Merrymeeting scull boat held two people — a sport in the bow and the guide steering in the stern. You'd set your decoys out in the grass and lay back 400 yards to watch the ducks land. The trick was to scull the boat in amongst the decoys without letting those birds know you're there.

"What we'd do was to 'brush up' the boat with drift grass and alders. Then we'd lie on our backs. The guide's head would be supported just high enough above the gunwale to see over it. His feet lay by the sport's head. If the man in the bow was a right-shouldered shooter, the butt of his gun was under his right arm and across his chest. The dog would sit somewhere in between, poised and quietly waiting.

"The guide would scull up to the birds. If it's a little rough out, you catch sudden glimpses of the birds, and your heart starts to thump. All the while you're wondering if you'll have the chance to get in shooting range. If you do, the guide yells, 'SIT UP.'

"An experienced gunner will sit right up and nail puddle ducks, mallards, widgeons, pintails, blue wing wood ducks, and black ducks — whatever is swimming among the decoys. Those ducks will hit the water with their wings, kick with their feet, and spring straight up a few feet off the surface of the water before they start to fly. It takes them a little time to get going and in those few seconds, the gunner goes to work.

"Back in the 1930's on Merrymeeting Bay, there was a 10 bird limit. You could use live decoys as opposed to those made of cork or wood. We bred those decoys for the purpose. We took noisy, talkative, English call ducks and crossed them with big, tame, rouen ducks. Then we bred in some wild black duck blood. The result was a tame, noisy, large black duck that we called 'Judas birds.'

"We put a strand around the leg of the live decoy with gangions, and snapped about eight female ducks into rings attached to a trawl line which we anchored at one end. Then we anchored one drake on the other side of a bunch of bullrushes where the female ducks can't see him. The females will talk back and forth with the drake, and this chatter helps bring in the wild ducks. Or you'd release the drake, and let him swim in among the females.

"Next you'd scull down to the tame decoys who know you're there. When they see you comin' they get down low in the water, but wild ducks don't pay attention to this. Once you're in range, you sit up, jump the wild birds, and shoot as many as you can.

"Some sports were poor shots. It became the job of the guide to sit up when they weren't looking and shoot simultaneously to bring down a few. The sport thinks that he did it, and everyone leaves happy.

"Conservationists had live decoys outlawed. They claimed we were shooting down too many birds. We pointed out that there was a bag limit, and that cork decoys didn't bring in as many birds at close range, and that more hunters were crippling ducks with long shots. It's a shame. Live decoys were to the experienced duck hunter what hound dogs were to rabbit, coon, and fox hunters, and what bird dogs were to quail and woodcock hunters. The dogs haven't been outlawed.

"The use of bait was also outlawed, but for better reasons. You'd dump a 100-pound bag of corn feed out in a straight line for 30 feet, and line your guns up behind a tree. I have seen two guns fired in a snow storm at night, and 76 birds bite the dust.

"I used to hunt out of Duxbury, Massachusetts. There on the marshes we had a hunting lodge — a cabin with a bunk room, kitchen, and pantry — 80 feet long and 24 feet wide. We used to send out fliers.

"We'd keep 225 goslings and yearlings in our pens. We kept them hungry during the day and would feed them at night. Then we'd tether their fathers to the beach on the north, and their mothers on the beach to the south. The beach in the middle we kept open.

"When we saw a flock of geese approaching, we'd liberate 200 fliers. They'd form flock formations to lure the geese in. In the meantime, their fathers and mothers on the beach would be calling them to come back. Hungry, they'd return with the wild birds not far behind, and light on the beach in the middle where we placed feed. We'd often get the entire team of fliers back in three minutes.

"When the wild geese came down, we tried to shoot the ganders. If you kill the gander in a flock, the goose will bring the yearlings and goslings back looking for him. You see, they marry for life. If you kill the goose, the gander will round up his flock, and get the hell out of there. I have seen four hunters down 40 out of 41 geese using this method. Few birds get away crippled.

"To me, hunting with a dog is what puts the frostin' on the cake. I love working with dogs. You become a team. When I'm on a hunting trip, instead of leaving the dog in the car at night, I don't have my head on the pillow very long before the dog's in right beside me. The old-timers taught me that you have to treat the dog with kindness and respect. You don't know things the dog does and vice versa, so you depend on each other. They have good natural instinct and common sense.

"A trained Labrador will sit outside your blind very quietly, watching and waiting. He may turn his head just a little, or his ears may come up, and his tail wag slightly — but he can be taught to remain steady as a rock until after you've shot. At your command, he'll retrieve.

"One day I left two sports in a blind on the marsh. When I returned, they had shot a bird in the air with his wings set. He scaled across the river into a pine tree a quarter of a mile away. I had to line up my dog for a blind retrieve.

"In a blind retrieve, the dog doesn't know where the bird is. You have to aim him in the right direction with a line. The line goes right between his shoulder blades, up over the top of his head, and ends at the tip of his nose. You motion the direction of the line with your arm and tell the dog, 'Back.' A good dog will take the command and follow that line. If he gets off center, you whistle. He'll look back for directions so you tell him, 'Over . . . back,' with your arm movements.

"Dogs will swim to the other side of river banks in any kind of weather. If they're experienced, they stop, turn around, and look at you asking, 'Okay,

I've got this far. What do I do now?'

"You keep motioning, 'Back,' and he'll take the line. You may motion, 'Back-over.' That means go at a 45-degree angle. And they do it.

"Once the dog is in the area of the downed bird, his nose goes to work. He'll find that duck, softmouth it, swim back across the river, bound across the marsh, and hold up the duck for you to take, wagging his tail. It's beautiful.

"Some dogs will button-hook. They learn that a downed bird may only be crippled and will crawl off downwind. A dog who beelines straight for where a duck dropped may miss him upwind. But a dog who zigs downwind slightly will get scent of him.

"You know, dogs can think. I once had some sports who were bad shots. We split up, and I gave a dog to one. The sport sat down by the water, and some diving fowl flew by. The sport was shootin' and missin', and the dog was watchin'. Eventually the dog quit the sport and came back to me.

"One dog was a regular clown. A sport was squatting by a little pond. After he missed a few shots like that, this dog went over to him and licked his nose. Then he put both paws on the sport's shoulders, knocked him backwards into the water and ran like hell out of there, smiling.

"I used to be friendly with George Soule. He is pictured in some of L.L. Bean's catalogs — he made their duck decoys by hand for years. We were gunning at a license trial in Pittsfield one season. In one of the events, they were popping birds into the air for the co-captains to shoot. Well, they were having a bad day and missing a lot. There were many fly-aways, and I was teasing one guy I knew for 25 years about it.

"That afternoon, Soule and I were up at bat. We went over and asked the co-captains if we could use 20-gauge guns. They must have been a little irritated with their morning fly-aways and my joking 'cause one says, 'You can use any damn gun you want, but just as soon as you miss a bird — you're done.'

" 'You mean we can keep shooting as long as we hit 'em?' I asked.

"They nodded their heads, and smirked. You see, normally, you change hands every eight birds in a 62 bird event.

"So we got out there. Six birds were thrown up, and we shot six birds down for the dogs to retrieve. Some birds slipped out of the thrower's hands by accident. We downed them. We were lucky and soon, after 62 clean kills, it was over. We had shot the whole event without a single fly-away. Never in the history of the Maine License Field Trials had anyone heard tell of this.

Most felt that we couldn't concentrate long enough to shoot 10 birds.

"So here we were, two old-timers, you know? We weren't all dressed up pretty with feathers in our caps or anything. As we were walking out, George turns to me and whispers, 'Well Ransom, guess we're gettin' a little age on us, but I think we can still show 'em something.' We got a hell of a kick out of that."

"Guiding and duck hunting has changed a lot since the times when I first went out with Erle Browne. Gunning has gone from a sport to a field day. People don't respect the birds or each other anymore. A lot of guys will go out into a field, get roaring drunk, and shoot at their empty beer cans which they throw in the Bay. They'll call out, 'Here ducky ducky,' and shoot when the birds are out of range. The ducks have caught on and now fly in huge flocks. Try and decoy one duck out of 1,000. There's survival in large numbers, and the ducks know it. Also, they'll go out and sit in the ocean now, only to return at night to feed.

"The problem is that there are few guides left; no one wants to hire them. Young fellows starting out today have no guide or old-timer to show them how it's supposed to be done; they have no role model. Sixteen-year-olds grow up with hunting licenses and no training. It's horrible and sad.

"Anyway, the guiding I've done in my lifetime has allowed me to meet some very fine people. There's a lot of satisfaction in guiding some city slicker who's been on the treadmill too long. They show up here nervous wrecks, chain-smoking and drinking. You get these guys out in the open, and they relax some. By the end of the week, they go home at peace with themselves and with the world. And that's wonderful."

EDWARD LAMBERT

Greenville

"I KNEW THAT *if ever I was to be a Maine guide, I was going to have to learn to shoot a gun. So I went off into the woods, found some old-timers sittin' in their cabin, and asked them if they'd teach me. One of 'em handed me a gun, pointed to some rabbit tracks, slapped me on the back, and pushed me off saying, 'At the end of them tracks is your dinner.'*

" 'But aren't you going to teach me how to use this gun?' I asked.

"Well, they mumbled something like, 'Experience is the best teacher,' and as I started off, I could hear they was laughin' up a storm.

"Well, I hadn't gone more than 100 yards when I heard some gobbling overhead, and there was 12 turkeys settin' up on a tree branch. I took aim, closed my eyes, and squeezed off a shot. The bullet split the branch down the middle, catching all 12 turkeys by their feet before snapping closed again. I ripped off the branch with them birds, slung it over my shoulder, and hadn't gone more than another 100 yards when I heard an awful roarin' sound.

"It was a grizzly bear, charging. I didn't even have time to shoulder the gun so I stood my ground. When he got near, I shoved my hand into his open mouth, down his throat, through his intes-tines and out the other end. Then I reached up, grabbed a hold of his tail, and gave it a YANK. I turned the bear inside out.

" 'Course, he kept on a-going, but it was in t'other direction.

"Well, I hadn't gone more than another 100 yards, still following those rabbit tracks, when I spied two foxes on a river bank. I could see they was mean, rabid foxes, and they was going to bite me if they could. Then I heard some wicked honking and

quackin'. I looked up, and there was seven geese flying south, and seven ducks flying north. 'Course, I decided to take on the danger first.

"I had only one bullet left. I took aim somewhere in between them foxes, not knowin' which one to shoot at, and squeezed the trigger. The gun exploded, and the bullet sped true to its mark, hit a rock, and split the rock in two, killing both foxes. The butt of the rifle flew north and knocked down all seven ducks. The barrel flew south and skewered all seven geese. The recoil of the explosion sent me flying into the stream, and when I come to, my right hand was on an otter's head, my left hand was on a beaver's tail, and my pants pockets was so full of trout that a button popped off my fly and killed the rabbit.

"That's what you call beginner's luck."

— MARSHALL DODGE, traditional story.

EDWARD LAMBERT *had beginner's luck. He spent his life as a trapper, guide, and Spencer Mountain fire-watch. With experience as his teacher, he learned much about Dame Nature.*

Beneath Lambert's insulating surface of emotional reserve are gentle compassion and humility. His beagle looks up at him with languid eyes, returning affection. Lambert blends respect for animals with profound understanding of human nature.

Lambert is pensive. He speaks softly and deliberately, pausing only to attend to his pipe. Turning it upside down, he knocks out some charred tobacco against the top of the parlor stove. He reloads its contents using his thumb as a stuffer. He runs his hands through crew cut, gray hair and then rekindles his conversation.

EDWARD LAMBERT / *Greenville*

"I WAS BORN IN BANGOR IN 1911 and was four years old when my father died. My grandfather adopted me, and I lived with him on his father's farm at the edge of the wilderness in Hancock County. I remember my great-grandfather. He was a big man some seven axe-handles tall, and he didn't have to turn around twice to cast a shadow. When he come home, he cleared himself a farm. That's where we lived.

"Well son, in 1931 during the Great Depression, I had come home from

school, and kid-fashion, went snoopin' around the attic. I found an old trunk of my great-grandfather's, and in it were these old logging maps of the Pistol Lakes where he'd lumbered.

"I'd never heard of them lakes before, and no one else had either. Since the maps was poor, I vowed to rediscover these lakes. It was around that time that me and my cousin got word that they was payin' 25 cents a piece for a pair of young porcupine. We quit our jobs which was payin' 75 cents a day and went off trappin'. While we was at it, we tried to find them Pistol Lakes.

"Before leavin', we found an old-timer and asked him if he ever heard of them lakes. He said they struck a distant chord, and directed us into the country around the Nickatowah Stream. We went up-country on his advice and spent the year in those waters. Sure enough, we rediscovered them lakes where the loggers used to camp. The fact that there were from four to six pound salmon and trout there didn't discourage us a bit.

"It had been almost 100 years since Man had been in that region. The animals hadn't learned to fear us and had multiplied. We could walk right up to deer and they'd just stand there, lookin' at us. Partridge and grouse were runnin' around our feet. And I never saw such white perch in all m'life. They'd run five pounds and busted all present-day records to pieces. All we did was throw in a baited line and reel it in, and a big black wake would follow close behind.

"We built ourselves a log cabin by some old trails we found by a lake. We also built a log cache for our fur and supplies, and then spent the winter trappin'. We didn't know nothing about trapping when we started, but it didn't matter. All we had to do there was to stand on the side of a stream for a while to see an otter slide by or catch a mink playin' on shore. We ended up makin' three dollars a day, and that was a fortune for us durin' the Depression."

"The whole secret to trappin', son, is you've got to know what the animal is goin' to do *before* he does it. Only then can you get your trap in the right place. Now, what I advise these young kids who come to me to learn is to wait for the first snowfall, and then go and pick up an animal track, say of a coyote. Spend the whole day followin' that track. Notice what that coyote eats, how he hunts, and what kind of terrain he travels in.

"Once you've learned the habits of the animal, you know where to set your traps. Say that coyote is catchin' mice. Watch how he digs them out of holes. Look at the tracks he made. Then, when you set your trap, make it look like a coyote had been diggin' there and put in a mouse scent. When other animals see that, they'll just figure that the coyote didn't want to eat that mouse then, and buried it. You see, animals love to steal from each other. They get something they don't want at the time, they'll bury it. Another animal will come along and paw it out again. And when he does, he'll pay the price and step into your trap.

"Coyote is my favorite animal to trap. They're the smartest things on four legs. They're scavengers that will eat everything from garbage to rabbits and apples. I've spent weeks studyin' them.

"When you trap a coyote, approach him with caution. A fox caught in a trap will thrash and jump and try to free himself. A coyote will just lay down flat and be still, camouflaged in the snow. When you finally see them, maybe five feet away, their lips are all curled back. They're the size of a 60-pound German shepherd and powerful. They can drag a trap through brush that two husky men couldn't get through, and they can break your arm in their jaws. So I'm cautious.

"Bobcats are easier to catch. I just make a little brush house and place some bait in the back of it. The trap is in front.

"Bobcats can't smell so good, but they have sharp vision. When they see something movin', they get curious. I've seen them sneak up on a piece of birch bark blowin' in the wind. They probably thought it was a deer's tail. So I caught on. I hung a little white piece of cloth on a tree near the trap. Lured one in range of the bait scent, and got him.

"Another technique I learned was in huntin' deer. Never follow a deer track in snow. Keep swingin' out to the sides and then comin' back. You see, deer travel into the wind so that if there's anything in front, they'll get a whiff of it. Their nose tells them of danger. And their eyes, set on the sides of their head, watch that back trail close to see if anyone is following. There's so many bobcats and coyotes on their tracks that this habit is inbred. And now, it's Man on their tracks.

"Anyway, if you leave the deer track and circle, plenty of times you'll catch that deer standing there lookin' back at his tracks. He wouldn't even know you're around.

"Now when I was a kid, I was taught to 'Kill what you need and be damn sure you need what you kill.' If the Old Man wanted four partridges, you got four bullets. If you didn't follow a wounded deer through the woods as long as was humanly possible, the Old Man worked you over with a razor strap.

We were taught only to shoot when we could aim for a vital spot. None of this runnin' through the woods like you see now, shootin' at every songbird and chipmunk that comes along. We hunted animals 'cause we needed the meat. Never for sport.

"Unfortunately, the average hunter today sees an animal and just shoots a bullet. If the animal doesn't drop right there, the heck with it, he'll go off and look for another. It's disgusting to find the number of deer dead and dyin' with gunshot wounds.

"I remember the open seasons we had on moose in Oxford County. It was the most disgustin' mess I ever seen — worse than the Battle of the Bulge. You didn't straighten up 'cause somebody would shoot ya. You were only supposed to shoot bulls, which is no sport since they just stand there lookin' at you. Well, there was cows layin' everywheres — some just left there to rot.

"Man is the most dangerous animal there is.

"Now roughly 45 years ago, you weren't allowed to trap beaver 'cause they had been pretty near wiped out. So the first time I ever saw a beaver stump on Madagasket Stream, I didn't know what it was. Here was this stump all chawed around and comin' to a peak. I cut it off and brought it home to show my grandfather.

" 'What's this?'

" 'Good lad, that's a beaver cut. I haven't seen one for years and years!'

"So we went back to the stream and sneaked around it until we found this pair of small beaver. They was tryin' to put in a dam, but the current was strong, and they kept gettin' swept away. We watched, and soon thought we'd lost our beaver — but four weeks later I was down there fishin' and see'd they was back.

"I told Gramps, and we snuck back again to watch. What had happened was the pair of young beavers had gone downstream to fetch an old beaver. And he was BIG! You know, a beaver is the only animal that will keep on growin' as long as it lives. A Canadian chap did a study on beavers and found that their growth is controlled by their feedin' habits. If the feed gets scarce in a certain locality, the females will just stop breedin', or just have one pup. Wolves do the same thing. Don't ask me how they do it. Man is smart enough to go to the moon, but he can't figure that one out. I also learned from this Canadian chap who studied beaver fossils that thousands of years ago, the beaver grew to be the size of our present day bear. The trees he gnawed upon were also huge.

"Anyway, these two young beavers was havin' trouble holdin' down the dam they was tryin' to make, so they fetched this big old fella. He must have been the head engineer 'cause they put a dam in, the remains of which, as far as I know, are still there to this day. He must have come up there with his tools and showed them where to anchor.

"I do all my trappin' for beaver under the ice in winter. I just cut a hole and lay in a piece of poplar which they like to eat. They'll be swimmin' along their runs, which are certain areas that they'll travel. You have to watch 'em to find out where these runs are, or you wouldn't know where to place your trap.

"The beaver will be swimmin' along, and he'll see this piece of poplar that you've anchored in the middle of his run. He'll think one of the boys dropped it and will grab it. When he finds it wouldn't budge, he'll swim down along the line as far as he can and try to cut it off from the bottom. While he's cuttin' it free, his feet is tucked up into his chest, but when he grabs it, he puts his feet down on the bottom. If your trap is set in the right place — you've got him!

"Beavers will grow and live quite a while, but the casualty rate among them is pretty high. Trappers, coyote, and bear kill a lot of them, and even bobcats will catch 'em when they're buildin' their dams. Also, there are a lot of accidents where a beaver has either dropped a tree on himself or on another fella. They cut the trees off and run away, but they don't know where it's gonna fall and may run in the wrong direction.

"Years ago when I was guiding, I'd be talkin' with sports who planned to come back up huntin' in the fall. I would ask 'em if they'd like to have a bear. Well, they always would.

"They'd go home, and my cousin and I would make a big bear trap. We'd build a big cubby about four feet high and three feet wide out of dried brush. It didn't have to be solid. A bear or a bobcat will do anything to keep from steppin' on a twig which might snap, so by buildin' with dried brush, they'd ease right in through the cubby openin'. I used to take big patches of moss and make places for 'em to step on so they could sneak up quietly on the bait at the rear of the cubby. Underneath one of those moss patches would be a bear foot trap hooked to a toggle and a weight. The point wasn't to hold the creature but to slow him down as he ran and fought the trap and got hung up in everything that came in his way. There's no holdin' anything the size of a bear anyway.

"Then you overtake him and shoot him. We'd shoot usin' a .22 revolver which didn't mark up the hide. Then we'd dress 'em out, and take 'em down to Bangor to put into cold storage.

"For an extra $25, we'd throw in the story of how the sport shot his bear. They could shoot a hole in him later anywhere they wanted, and we could make up a spicy tale to fit. Like the sport seeing the bear out of the corner of his eye, whistling to catch his attention, the bear rears up, the sport shoots over his shoulder — anything! City slickers back home don't know the difference anyway!

"Our bear trap itself used to be a set of clamps with two springs. You'd wind one spring and then the other. To pry it open, you kept at a stick's distance.

"Nowadays they have Conibear 'killer-traps' which I like very much. All of the boys do. An animal steps into one of them and BAM — they're dead. The springs come together on a wire mechanism, and it breaks the animal's neck. It's so fast that if you threw a pencil and it hit the wire, the pencil would be broken in half before it hit the ground. You never use this kind of trap alone since it can break a man's arm before you know it. It takes two men to loosen it. That's a trap you've got to show a lot of respect for.

"I carry a .22 revolver when I tend my traps. A lot of trappers take a club and stun whatever is in their trap or stand on the creature's heart. I don't. If I got to dispatch of an animal, I like to do it just as quick and merciful as I can. By usin' .22 bullets, it makes just a small hole through the skull. The bullet enters the brain and kills them instantly. No pain. No mark. That's the only thing I don't like about trappin' — to find something alive in my trap. That's why I like these killer traps. There's no need to finish off an animal with them. You know it was killed instantly and didn't stay there sufferin'.

"Now, I guess you think we make the animals suffer in traps. Well, actually an animal caught in a trap is not in agony — he's just mad 'cause he's caught. It's something strange to him. It's just like puttin' a leash and collar on a dog for the first time. He'll fight it like hell for a little while 'til he realizes he's not being hurt, and the shock wears off. And the trap *doesn't* hurt. It cuts off all of the blood circulation so there's no pain. You can put a clamp down on your hand and in no time at all, it'll just be all numb. If that blood doesn't run through there, feelin' goes.

"You've had your foot go to sleep, haven't ya? Well, think of that, only 10 times as numb, and you see that you could cut off a toe and never know it.

"The environmentalists show photographs of skunks caught in traps chewin' off their feet to escape. Well, what's really happenin' is that the skunk is tryin' to bite off the trap, only he misses and bites below it without knowin' he's chewin' off his foot 'cause there's absolutely no feelin' in his toes. If he does free himself, then I've no doubt there's considerable sufferin' when the circulation returns to the point where the toes are gone. But most of the time they never get that far."

"Maine may be the last frontier in the Northeast. Your grandchildren and mine will never know what it used to be like. Twenty years ago on a clear day on Spencer Mountain, all you could see for 100 miles was wilderness. No roads. No houses. No signs of greed.

"Today I look, and Great Northern has the Golden Road cutting through Greenville to Baxter Park in Millinocket. The road is full of hunters and fishermen and the dead bodies of moose who got hit. The country has changed so much, it's enough to make you sick. And Man is upsetting the balance of Nature by trying to regulate hunting seasons and coyotes. They've forgotten that Nature can take care of itself. If any animal gets too thick, mange and disease set in, and they starve. It's pitiful, and the trappers and hunters can prevent some of it. But still, Nature shouldn't be tampered with too much.

"You know, life is a routine of long hard days and cold stormy nights, son. Remember them Pistol Lakes I was talkin' about? Well, I hadn't been back for a long time when I met my cousin. We talked over old times, and them lakes came up.

"He told me, 'Don't go back.' He told me don't go back 'cause the paths we helped to swamp out are now a highway they're usin' to ride into with Cadillacs. He told me don't go back 'cause the little log cabin is a hotel. He told me don't go back 'cause there's no fish left in them streams and no game left in those woods. He told me don't go back 'cause Man had returned."

CHARLES COE

Greenville

THE GLASSY SURFACE OF MOOSEHEAD LAKE *disappears into the fog, muffling the eerie call of a solitary loon. Charlie Coe, a bush pilot, is grounded. He sits in the hangar, joking with the other bush pilots. Outside is a Canadian Beaver — the aerial workhorse of the North.*

Finally the weather clears. Coe straps a canoe onto one of the Beaver's pontoons, tosses in a rucksack, and seats his passengers. In one fluid motion he unhooks the hawser, pushes the Beaver from the dock, and climbs into a worn leather chair. He checks the rudder and elevators, throttles the radial engine, and the Beaver roars to life in a burst of blue smoke. Vibrations shudder through the plane as it builds speed into the wind, bouncing off ripples until it breaks contact with the lake.

Airborne, Coe watches Greenville disappear from sight. Views of Mount Katahdin and Squaw open into an Allagash horizon — a dark mass of spruce, bogs, and rivers that snakes into Canada.

"There's a moose!" yells Coe above the droning engine. He points out the open cockpit window at a bull grazing knee-deep in an inlet. Suddenly the world tilts as Coe banks in for a closer look. Passengers' stomachs are heaved into their throats as the plane dives. Pointing the nose back up into a steep climb, they sense nausea from adrenal recession. Air sickness bags are close at hand. Flying with bush pilots is nothing like some staid jaunt in a vast 747.

CHARLIE COE / *Greenville*

"I WAS BORN IN PORTLAND IN 1922. I was interested in flying since the time I was a little kid. Instead of playing with toys in the sand, I built model airplanes. When World War II broke out, they needed pilots really bad. So at age 19, I joined the Army Air Force. I learned to fly in the Steerman, a biplane. Later I flew Flying Tigers and Mustangs on patrols to defend our bombers.

"After the War, I got my instructor's rating and learned to fly seaplanes. I've been here in Greenville flying out of Moosehead Lake since 1947.

"We're bush pilots. We fly away from the congested airports into the woods and wilderness. We can land on ponds from Maine to Alaska. That's where you find most of us.

"When I first became involved with bush flying, I thought of commercial pilots who landed on the ground in Bridgeport, Connecticut as being small-time stuff. We're bush league, so to speak — the best pilots. There's a greater challenge on the frontier.

"Up here, you're on your own. It's that old barnstorming spirit. You don't have Federal Aviation Authority (FAA) rules and radio regulations to follow. You don't have to wait for permission to take off or land. You have to use your common sense.

"You know, in the 1920's and 1930's, all of the pilots who survived World War I wanted to keep flying. There weren't many airports; it was still the beginning of aviation. So they'd buy an old Jenny, fill it with gas, and take off for the Midwest. There they'd land by barns and farms, hence the name barnstorming. They'd do a few roll maneuvers and stunts to get interest up, and then offer rides to the locals. That paid for their gas. Then they'd jump back in their planes and fly on to the next town. It was a life of tremendous freedom. It was these barnstormers who eventually started the airline companies.

"In the winter we take off on skis. We haul in cross-country skiers and trappers into the Allagash. There's a danger of whiteouts. That's when the snow is white, the ground is white, and you can't see the horizon. You can

get vertigo, and the altimeter isn't of much use. When you're flying through mountain passes, you never know sometimes when the skis will touch the ground. Those conditions have killed a lot of pilots. We try to avoid them.

"In summer we're a flying taxi service for sports who want to get into remote hunting and fishing camps. We'll carry everything: stoves, canoes, camping gear, and supplies.

"The Beaver is indispensible. When I first got here, we flew planes that only went about 70 miles per hour. It took me two hours to make one trip into the Allagash. I could only make two trips seating two people, and it was expensive. Today, the Beaver sits four passengers and can fly at 125 miles per hour. It takes me a little over an hour to make one round trip into the Allagash. And it's cheaper — maybe $20 on the average.

"We play around when we can. Like any American boy, I used to enjoy what you might call stunts. I once took Harry Sanders III up. He wasn't airsick or anything so I did a loop. Still looked okay, so I did a snap roll, a slow roll, and put her into a spin. Harry was still grinnin'. Then I did an Immelmann roll — a half loop that flattens out again on top. Never did faze Harry.

"Perhaps the most exciting thing is to fly people over Mount Kineo. It's a steep 1,789 feet high peak over Moosehead Lake. One side of it is a sheer concave cliff. I'd come at it over the opposite face of the mountain and fly along the plateau at the top over the cliff. As I go over, I'd bank the plane sharply, just over the edge. You're looking down, and there's ground 150 feet below you. All of a sudden, there's the lake — ZAM — down 1,789 feet below. It's a spectacular sight. Makes flying up here worthwhile."

JOHN MORSE

Winnegance

Morses *have populated the banks of the Kennebec River for seven generations, cutting and processing trees. John Morse is the latest in this family line. His somber face is pinched with cold as he explains that there is "nothing romantic" about logging. "It's muddy work. You get bug-bitten. Pine needles are always falling down your sweaty neck. You get skinned knuckles, twigs in your eyes, bruised shins, cricks in your neck, and aches in your back." Morse plunges his hands deep into the pockets of his wool trousers and shrugs snow off his shoulders. "Most of all, it's not fun."*

Morse is a substantial man who has seen the ice flow out of the Kennebec River more than 60 times. He speaks in a soft, mellifluous voice that contrasts with the raucous buzzing of chain saws of his mill. His humor is dry as sawdust; his memory as sharp as a blade.

JOHN MORSE / *Winnegance*

"I WAS BORN IN 1918 IN BATH, the home of my ancestors. I suppose that I've got one foot in the grave and the other one standing on a cake of soap. I went to a one-room schoolhouse and then to Morse High School where I graduated in 1936. From there I went right into my father's lumber business.

"You've got to be a damn fool to get into the lumber business. My wife tells me I got into it 'cause I didn't know any better. I think it was inertia, and now I haven't got brains enough to quit.

"There's nothing to lumbering. You go in, look around, and what do you know — there's a tree. And this thing in my hand here is a saw. And when the two go together, you've got the business, a labor-intensive, capital-intensive headache.

"Of course, when I started out, we didn't have chain saws. We used cross-cut saws with handles on either end. Hopefully you and your partner didn't drag each other too much. When you got home, you felt like your guts were coming out the front of your shirt.

"Before the time of chain saws the lumber industry was a different kind of life. In the summer the mills were runnin' full steam. Many of the loggers stayed with their families on the farms or worked in the mills. In fall the men would harvest the crops and then take off for the woods. Their wives and children wouldn't see them again for three months.

"My father was in those logging camps. He said it was pretty rough. The camps were made of hand-hewn trees. They were inaccessible to the rest of the world. Teams of horses brought supplies in on sleighs, and a lot of food was shot right at the campsite. Game was more plentiful then.

"The loggers went out before daylight to arrive at the cutting sites by sun-up. To ship the logs from the forests to the rivers, teams of huge Clydesdale workhorses would haul them. You'd clasp down on the binder pole, and the caked snow would fly from the hooves over the wiffletree. It was nice, but hard, tiring work. When the men got back to the camps, their only desire was to eat all they could hold and get some shuteye.

"In spring the best sawyers would go to work on the river drives. They were chosen by the foremen (keymen). The drives on the Machias River were only four weeks in duration, but on the Kennebec, the drive used to start just as soon as the paper companies were relatively certain that freshets had passed.

"Ice on the rivers is a fearful subject. When it thawed and started moving out to sea, there was no stoppin' it. The ice would sweep everything before it with explosive cracking sounds and power.

"Before Wyman Dam was built below Moosehead Lake, the rules of the Scott Paper Company were that logs had to be securely piled on the river banks until the company asked for them. Sometimes the company misjudged, and a whole drive of logs would be caught in a freshet and swept out to sea. It wasn't unusual for pole cats to fall off the logs as they rode them by jams.

They'd be crushed to death. I tell you, it's a rough business.

"I witnessed the last of the log drives on the Kennebec River. The log drives simply consisted of putting the logs into the upper part of the river and then running down to the lower end of the river to sit on a rock and watch for them to come down. Of course that's a little over-simplified, because the sons-of-bitches hang up on the sandbars, rocks, dams, bridge piers, and everything else along the way down.

"The log drives continued until 1972, but the long log drives ended 40 years earlier. You see, one of the things a log company needed was boom logs which were chained together to guide the rest of the logs along, and to stop them when necessary. Boom logs worked just like a corral that held in horses. Under the rules of the drive, the companies could pick any log out of the river that they wanted to use as long as they recorded it and told the proprietor paper companies. Of course the drivers always picked the best and longest logs. Much of the best spruce was lost along the way.

"Then you'd get a bunch of logs hung up on a ledge somewhere and, well boys, hand me a few sticks of dynamite and we'll take care of that . . . .

"Dynamite was used to free up log jams where a lot of the creatures piled up. Other ways to free up the jams were to move in a steam donkey and use it to haul the beasts out, one by one, until they could start the jam moving again. But this was difficult and more time consuming. It caused a man to want to give up drinking due to frustration, so dynamite was used.

"With dynamite, the long logs would get broken up, and the pulp wood flew all around. Often you ended up with match sticks instead of a long log, and many larger chunks were blasted into Grandpa Jones' field where they couldn't be moved again.

"Then you'd wonder why you didn't take out as many long logs at the end of the drive as you put in at the beginning. The answer was usually lying along the river banks.

"Another reason for stopping the long log drives was the damage that the logs were doing to the river. When a log was put in at Lake Moscow in May and taken out of the river at Hallowell in October it had been bounced, dragged, scraped, rolled, and tumbled all the way. By then most of the bark had come off. In theory the Kennebec is paved in some places with many feet of bark (which sinks).

"Still, I don't buy the theory that this was doing the river a great deal of harm. I don't think that it's doing anywhere near as much harm as the tons and tons of chemical pollutants that paper and textile mills were putting into the river, or the thousands of tons of raw sewage that towns and cities dump in.

"Nevertheless, that was one of the issues that helped to stop the drives. Ecologists said the bark made it difficult for marine organisms (which fish eat) to thrive. Ecosystems were hurt.

"The paper companies would have also liked to have continued the river drives. When they gave them up, a lot of people regretted it. I guess that they didn't realize all of the ramifications. For one thing, the road from Jackman to Skowhegan is a rather crooked and narrow highway. Now, every 90 seconds, one of Scott Paper Company's loaded, trailer tractor trucks goes spinning by on two wheels all along the road, day and night. They carry a great load of logs, tree length, piled up as high as they can and still be able to clear the bridges. The drivers are paid by the load, and not by the hour. So you can imagine the traffic and accident toll is pretty severe. Still, transporting the logs was always dangerous work, I guess.

"The Scott Paper Company had its origins in a man named Milton G. Shaw. M.G. Shaw was a farmer up in Greenville and started out with very little. But Shaw was a crusty old character and had the foresight to see that there was a future in timberland investment. He deprived his family and himself to save every penny he could for acreage purposes. The timberland in the 1830's and 40's that he bought only cost 25 cents an acre. He was so thrifty that he wouldn't give his children the money to buy new shoes. In the winter, when the ground was frozen and there was snow on the ground, Shaw's son had to round up the cows in late afternoon to get them back into the barn before nightfall. His son's shoes were so worn out that he used to walk behind the cows in the droppings to keep his feet warm. But in time, M.G. Shaw became a fare-thee-well self-made man, and very wealthy.

"After M.G. Shaw had acquired his land, he came to Bath and started up the M.G. Shaw Lumber Company where the Bath Iron Works parking lot is now. He had a sawmill run by steam, and used the Kennebec River to ship his lumber to New York, Baltimore, and Boston.

"Despite the fact that Shaw became a millionaire, and one million dollars back then was probably the equivalent of 10 million dollars today, he used to work daily at the mill and help the sawyers make decisions like when to cut off a blemish of rot in a 20-inch board of pine.

"Now, the company's boom ran along the front of the river. Logs were chained together, and piles driven in to secure them. As the logs came down

the river from the drives up-river, the rafts were broken up, and the logs pushed into the boom corral.

"Evidently the mill received some kind of an order, and M.G. Shaw, being the worker that he was, was out on the boom with a pick pole selecting the logs to be guided into the mill. He contrived to fall overboard, and he couldn't swim any at all, or not much. Anyhow, he was foundering around in the water, and one of the guys from the mill saw him, ran down onto the boom, grabbed him, and dragged him back onto the log boom. Mr. Shaw was pantin' all out of breath and finally got his wind and looked up at the guy and says, 'You damned fool — if you'd been payin' attention to your work you wouldn't of seen me!'

"Another time, Mr. Shaw and a logger named Charles Talbot went up to the North Woods country to cut some timber. In those days the mills didn't run in winter because no logs could be gotten through the ice down-river. Sometimes, after cutting the logs, they'd be piled up into big piles by the road-side up to 10 miles from the water. The hauling roads were concave, and iced, and huge horse-drawn sleds would take the logs down the road to the river bank. They would load double sleds with long, 50-foot logs and pile 'em up to 12 feet high.

"By this time M.G. Shaw was in his mid-60's and was watching his men rolling the logs up skids and onto the sleds to be taken to the river. Well, Charles Talbot was supervising and told this particular crew that they had piled enough logs on and gave the okay to take it away. Shaw stepped in and told them to pile on another few feet! Then, when he felt the time was right, he said, 'Okay Charles, bind 'er on and take it down to the landing.'

"Well, Charles didn't believe that the disproportionate load of logs, by now touching the bottom branches of trees overhead, could be moved. He said, 'Mr. Shaw, I think it would be a good idea if you tried to take it down.'

" 'Well, it ain't as if I couldn't, Charlie,' Shaw replied. And with that he got on the load, took his whip, beat the hell out of the horse team, and some-how got that sled started. Off he went over the horizon with Charlie standin' there by the side of the road, scratchin' his head.

"Shaw eventually sold his land and mill for another million dollars to what became the Scott Paper Company.

"You know, sawmills were an integral part of the shipbuilding process. A tremendous amount of timber went into the old schooners. They were heavier than steel vessels of comparable sizes. A medium-sized square-rigger with a 15-inch-thick hull of solid wood was quite formidable.

"My family used to cut wood, build ships, and then ship ice from the Kennebec River to all reaches of the world. That's what you call vertical integration.

"Once my father and I wandered over to the shipyard. One of the vessels on the trestles was pretty far along. My father went up for a closer look and lo and behold, his name was on the stern of her.

"My grandfather used to go to sea. Let me show you something. Here is a glass ball. It's not a crystal ball — it's a lightning rod that some genius sold to my grandfather.

"One of the hazards at sea on the square-riggers was the danger of being struck by lightning. There were some fierce storms in the tropics. The masts were 190 feet high in the open ocean and, after a sudden soaking in a squall, they made a perfect ground. Lightning immediately made for these masts.

"Well, my grandfather had the crew put some of these glass balls on the masts. He said he'd try anything once. A few months later, they ran into a squall. Well, the ball didn't ward off the lightning — it headed straight for the ship, struck the mainmast, and broke this ball off. As it fell, it gathered momentum. Went right through the deck of four-inch-thick pine planking and into the hold. Almost sunk the ship. My grandfather brought it home and muttered to my father that it really wasn't too effective.

"You know, at sea, medical attention was catch-as-catch-can. I heard about a man who sailed out of Bath tell how his skipper ordered a new medicine chest and doctor's book. He remembers one of the seamen coming aft and telling the captain, 'I've got an awful pain.'

"The skipper got out the doctor's book and tried to match the number on the bottles with the description of the sailor's ailment. He yelled to a seaman, 'Go down to my cabin and bring up the bottle in the medicine chest marked Number 12. I think that might cure this man.'

"The boy ran down, and minutes later stuck his head out the companion-way. He said, 'Captain, we haven't got any Number 12 left, but I'm bringing you two bottles of Number 6.' "

"You know, before the Carlton Bridge was built to Bath across the Kennebec, there used to be a ferry that ran from where the Bath Iron Works is to Woolwich. My uncle told me how there was a circus out east somewhere coming through Maine. For some reason, the elephants of the circus didn't take the railway but were walked over the roads. They got onto the ferry at Woolwich, but they wouldn't get off at the other side.

"Elephants are very knowledgeable about what will support their weight, and they were scared of the ramp leading from the ferry to the pier. Their elephant sense of ethics wouldn't allow them to budge. They just stood there, branting and pawing, with the men cajoling and pleading, and this went on for some time.

"It wasn't until the trainer figured out what the problem was that some men went to Percy and Small's shipyard for some stage plank. They reinforced the ramp with two layers of the stuff. Then the elephants willingly came into town."

"Frank Bowker was a shipbuilder down at Phippsburg center. They used to call him Deacon Bowker since he was also deacon of the church. He had a short white beard and hair, and he was a pretty spirited guy.

"In the early days of automobiles, the Deacon was a wildman with the car. I don't understand it, but it seems all of them old shipbuilders and sea captains were. They could thread a needle with a square-rigger, but they couldn't steer a straight line through a marked tunnel with a car.

"Well, Deacon Bowker bought a new car and wanted to show it off to his friends. He stopped over at Charles Maynard's general store and picked up a few of his cronies to give them a ride. They got to some sharp hairpin curves over by Parker Head. Just as they was going through the last of them curves, the Deacon yells, 'Hang on to your hats, boys — here we go.'

"Went right off the road into an apple orchard. They careened under the overhanging branch of a tree which ripped the roof and windshield completely off. They'd have been in trouble if they hadn't ducked in time.

"Another time, the Deacon was up at the corner of Front and Broad Streets in Bath. Evidently his foot reached for the accelerator when he meant to hit the brake. He unsuspectedly started off in reverse. This time, he backed right into the side of the Savings Institution going like a bat out of hell through the brick wall. He brought up with a terrible crash. The engine stalled and plaster was coming down. It was a mess. Somebody from the sidewalk peered in and said in a dry voice, 'Well Deacon, I see you've learned to park.'"

NELSON LEVASSEUR

Millinocket

MILLINOCKET *sprawls in the shadows of Mount Katahdin and the Great Northern Paper Company, its mill belching sulphurous steam into a pulpy, yellow sky. It is a company town rocked by the diesel rumbling of huge trucks carrying timber down Route 11, headlights blinking through the dust and haze.*

Nelson Levasseur is a company man. His French Canadian grandparents came into Maine to cut trees, drive them down the Penobscot, and to process them in the mill. He is stocky and rolls his cigarettes in callused hands. Narrowing his eyes, he drags in their smoke. He never seems to exhale and leaves long tips of ash dangling precariously. He tells what it's like to follow in Great Northern's logging tracks.

NELSON LEVASSEUR / *Millinocket*

"I've been around Millinocket all my life. Worked on the river drives on and off for 33 years and in the Great Northern mill for five years. I joined the labor force at age 15 by forging my papers and lying about my age. Then the working age was 16 and now it's 18. I never liked the mill — a peanut butter sandwich on the midnight shift wasn't for me. The woodlands were where I belonged.

"Millinocket is Great Northern. In 1941 there were only 5,000 people

[1 2 3

here. Now there's over 9,000 and we have the best of schools and a good town. Great Northern made it all in 80 years. And they own over 2.5 million acres of land which they cut selectively. It's huge but so's the demand for paper.

"In the old days the loggers used to walk into the logging camps along the telegraph wire cuts — sometimes plowing through snow clear over their waists. Ate the game they shot and lived off supplies stored on a wanigan boat that followed the loggers along the rivers. During the Depression eight hours of work a day fetched $1.00. The camps themselves were pretty rugged. Lots of lice, and the men slept outdoors. In the 1930's, the bed was a big long sheet of canvas attached to poles at either end. Bedding was fir boughs, and the blanket was a canvas tarp. You'd fold yourself up in it like an accordion. The same sheet covered as many as 150 men, 50 feet long. To keep warm, fires were posted along the length of the tarp about 10 feet apart.

"Them camps used to stink. Everyone ate beans and pea soup before camping down for the night. . . . As summer wore on and the weather got warmer, this long tarp would 'accidently' get cut off at either end and the men would go off into the woods for a better sleep. By the end of the summer the tarp was reduced to 150 sleeping bags.

"The men who worked on the river drives were mostly drifters off Bangor's 'Skid Row.' Skid Row referred to the men who skidded the logs down the river banks. Since they were often alcoholics, the term soon applied to down-and-outs in the downtowns of our cities like New York. A lot of these fellows were French Canadians, Scotch-Irish, 'Moosetowners' from Allagash, Finns, and Micmac Indians. Their fathers were often loggers with the Great Northern Paper Company since it started in 1902.

"When I was foreman for Great Northern, the first fellows I'd sober up in Bangor were the keymen — old-timers who knew their stuff. Professional river men. They'd help ready the camp with me in April and May. Then I'd round up some college boys, drivers, and pole cats, and we'd have a crew.

"I never really had any trouble with these crews. Once they were sobered up and underway, they were good men. We did have 'Jills' — fellows who didn't want to work, just get a good day's pay. We culled those guys out fast. And then there were 'Jillmocos' — fellows who worked for a spell, and got their pockets full of money that burned a hole in them. They'd get the down-river-cant and rumsick to get into town and go on a bender. They'd desert. If they made it into town somehow, as soon as they was broke, they was good men again and we'd get them back.

"Once we shipped out, there were few roads to return home on again. No one would see another streetlamp or Budweiser sign until they came down-river again in October. There was strong camaraderie among the men. You all worked together, slept together, and got drunk together. You had to get along on the rivers. In jams, your life depended on the other guy.

"Next, I'd get a good cook with me to help ready the logging camp. If you had yourself a good cook, you had yourself a crew. When there was a table, you had your place at it. Nobody sat in your place. And no talking was allowed. Just, 'Pass the meat. Pass the beans.' The paper companies furnished the grub by the time I was there. We'd load our supplies down here in Millinocket and truck the food up to Chesuncook dam. Then we'd ship it up-river 15 miles to some horse-drawn tote sleds which took it into the camps.

"Loggers were up for breakfast by 5:00 a.m. and they'd stay out working as long as there was light to see by. We ate four times a day. The food was hearty, and there was plenty of it; that's what we worked for. Lots of beans, ham, beef, pork chops, home-made bread, pies, cookies, peaches, pears, fish — everything.

"When the ice went out in spring we'd work the logs that we'd cut in winter down the Penobscot River to the mill. We'd also bring down the rear into Chesuncook Lake.

"Driving logs is similar to cattle drives in Texas. Out West cowboys chased the cattle from one ranch to another, hunted down strays, and branded them to keep track of whose they were. We done the same thing with logs.

"We worked in section crews of six men. Each crew worked a section of the river over a distance of 10 miles. In this way, lumber was kept moving down toward the mill.

"As the river rose and fell, log jams developed on rocks and snags. Peavymen and pole cats helped break up these jams. They'd ride the logs down with a pick pole for balance. It was dangerous work; a lot of men drowned or got crushed from falling off the logs. Bateaus were stationed downriver to rescue men who fell off and were washed downriver.

"To keep the logs moving down the streams, we used to construct horse dams which temporarily dammed up low sections of the rivers. In this way you could get up a head of water behind a gate which, when opened, would cause water to rush through with the logs.

"Once the logs reached Chesuncook Lake from the Penobscot River, a big tugboat with a crew of seven men would tow up to 4,000 cord of timber 20 miles. These logs were towed in long log booms. The booms were 28-foot-long logs chained together. One end of the log had a toggle and the other end had a ring. You'd marry the boom logs with a wooden peg. All our towing was governed by the wind. That's what pushed the logs from the river into the open boom. In 1946 we had to wait 25 days for a fair wind to come. During that time we went into Chesuncook village and played horseshoes or picked strawberries. There was nothing else to do.

"After the wood was towed to the other end of the lake, we'd haul the empty slack boom logs back up the lake to the mouth of the river and hang it up until the next load was due.

"When we finally got the logs down to the mill in Millinocket, we sorted them out into holding grounds. We used to hold 70,000 cord of wood there. After the drive was over, you'd get your pay. After being out for four months, even three dollars a day mounted up. Most of us would go into town and have a pretty good toot.

"Once in the mill, the logs had the bark removed and went through a system of sulphur and different chemicals that screen and clean the wood. Eventually, everything comes out the other end as paper.

"Since the river drives were banned, logging routes have been cut out for truckers. Like the 'Golden Road.' It's called that 'cause it cost so much to build. It follows the rivers down to the mill.

"Anybody who drives one of these trucks has to be a little crazy. I used to drive the trucks. They'd load on 25 cord of wood and haul them down unpaved roads at 40 miles an hour. It can get pretty hairy in spring and winter trying to slow down with a 70-ton load. In 1972, my diary records nine rollovers out of 60 trucks on the road. And the strain on the tires is terrible. I had two trucks in 1976 and had to pay $16,000 for tires alone. In one year. You have to be crazy to get into a business like that. It's a young man's game. That's why I got out."

ROBERT NEWELL,

MARY YARMAL,

DON STANLEY

Pleasant Point

You have noticed that everything an Indian does is in a circle,

and that is because the power of the world always works in

a circle, and everything tries to be round.

— BLACK ELK, *Black Elk Speaks*

THE PASSAMAQUODDY RESERVATION AT PLEASANT POINT *is a dreary, washed out, cinderblock town suffering from disrepair and depression. Dogs roam freely along muddy streets, there are sewage problems, and below the church, some men idle on the corner with bottles of wine in brown paper bags.*

The outlook for the natives is bleak but not hopeless. They have endured the degrada-

[1 2 9

tion of their culture for centuries. Then in 1975 an old trunk was discovered by Lena Brooks in the dusty attic of a house on the Princeton Penobscot Reservation. Inside was a yellowing treaty created by the United States Congress in 1790 called the Non-Intercourse Act. In the Act the federal government was set up to act as the Indians' trustee on matters involving the sale of land. White agents of the Indians violated this treaty, swindling land from them for over 100 years. Using this broken treaty as evidence in court, the natives of Maine filed a land claim. In 1980 the case was settled and the Indians received title to large tracts of forest, stumpage rights, and millions of dollars in compensation. Since that time they have been trying to rebuild their culture under the leadership of tribal governors such as Robert Newell.

Newell, Don Stanley, and Mary Yarmal are Passamaquoddies who voice their hopes and history.

Robert Newell, Mary Yarmal, Don Stanley /

Pleasant Point

"Do we consider ourselves Americans?" Mary Yarmal said with rhetorical cynicism in her voice. "No. I'm a Human Being and a Passamaquoddy Indian. The other things like 'American citizen' are there, but not for me personally."

"Those are tags," Don Stanley said. "I am also a Human Being from the Passamaquoddy Nation. A native from this country. I'm not an American. I will never be an American. I don't want to be an American."

"Back in history the Indians were put on reservations," Robert Newell said. "Back then it was to restrict them from being true Americans. Reservations were to restrict the Indians' movements. They made the Indian easier to manipulate; their land could be taken from them with great ease. The Indian had to stay on the reservation.

"Now the reservation has a totally different meaning. The Indian may come and go freely, but chooses to remain on reservation land. It is now his land. It is a symbol of what was once his. Out of reach of the white world, it is our home among brothers and sisters. It is a community where we can reserve our heritage."

"Boundaries are a white man's invention," Stanley said. "To the Indian, the Earth belonged to all the Human Beings and to the animals who lived there. Indians liked to move around. They used temporary shelters when on hunts following the fish and game. Home was not a reservation. It was where-ever the Indian happened to be.

"The Indian was here before the white man came over the oceans. His social life was far. His religion was far. The Indian was not a savage — he had a culture of his own. The white man refused to recognize this.

"The Indian was natural. He did things in accordance with the circle of life and was in harmony with the Creator and His Earth. Whenever Indians met, they met in a circle. Teepees were built on Mother Earth in a circle, un-like the square houses the Housing and Urban Development Agency would have us build. Lines are a white man's creation. They break the circle of power. The circle represents the cycle of life: the fish in the water, the birds in the air, and us, the Human Beings on the Earth.

"The non-Indian has somehow gotten away from the circle of life. He has set up his own system, and it is out of harmony with nature. He fights nature. He does not respect nature. He does not respect Mother Earth where we come from and return to.

"The Human Begins tend not to pollute the Earth. We don't throw gar-bage onto the Earth. We didn't dig mines, dump chemicals, or spill oil into the water. We didn't pollute the air — the air we breathe. All these things the Indian has to have.

"The white man is destroying the Earth, and therefore destroying him-self. He has so much advanced technology that he has found a way to destroy everything. And he will.

"I built my own house. It sits close to the Earth. I would sleep on the ground but that's hard to do in winter here. So I sleep on the floor which I built of logs and wood no more than 12 inches from the Earth. I can almost feel the warmth of the ground. In the new houses on the reservation we can't do this. They're built on cement foundations. They leak. It's terrible."

"I remember going hunting with my father," Yarmal said. "He never wasted any part of the animal. Every part would be used. He'd skin out the deer and dry its hide for clothes. The meat would be dressed and carved. We'd share it among the elders. The deer horns would be made into tools. The heels would be used for glue.

"The white hunters don't seem to think that way. I go into the woods and

see the animals they shot laying there without a head. Somebody killed them for sport so they could mock the animal and put its head on their wall. To the white man it's bravery and skill. To the Indian it's waste and sad disrespect for Mother Earth.

"An elder Indian once told me how the whites tried to get him to become Catholic. He came to church one day, and the priest asked why he never saw him on Sunday. The old man looked at the priest and said, 'I'm so sad that you can only find God one day a week when I have him all year long.'"

"The Indian had an unwritten code of ethics," Stanley said. "The white man has lost his feelings. He sets up bureaucracies with written rules and regulations. Even when he knows the laws are wrong or outdated, or cut against his feelings, he goes by the book. Everything is systematic from his games to the numerical grades children get in school. Everyone has so many numbers, statistics, and rules in white society.

"Somehow we Indians are also getting away from our traditional ways of government. Instead of a chief, we have a tribal governor. Our own offices are filling up with white man's red tape, so to speak."

"You don't know real discrimination until you know about the Indians," Yarmal said. "Black slaves were discriminated against in the South on the white man's land. The Indians were not brought here. This was our land. It was taken from us when Maine became a state in 1820. We were exploited by agents."

"Indian agents were white men who came onto the reservations," Stanley said. "They had outside interests in real estate, railroads, and in merchandising. Disobeying the Non-Intercourse Act of 1790, they acted on our behalf without the mediation of the federal government. It probably wouldn't have made too much difference since, at the time, the Bureau of Indian Affairs was under your War Department. The Indian didn't know how to read or write. Every time an agent wanted to bring forth a proposition, he'd do so on paper, and the Indian would be asked to add his mark."

"This embezzlement continued," Yarmal said. "In my lifetime, Maine was sending in agents who would offer us a grocery store. When we accepted, we found that we had to pay through an Eastport store. It had a monopoly on us. For a five dollar order we'd get three dollars worth of food, and the agent would pocket the rest. We once asked to look through this agent's files kept in Augusta. That was refused us. It was 'classified' information not available to the Indians.

"We pay income and state taxes, but we weren't allowed to send our children to public schools through the 1930's, and we weren't granted the right to vote until 1967. We were labelled 'wards of the state.' The white man made certain that we stayed that way by discriminating against us in the job market. We were kept on welfare deliberately.

"Recently we've been trying to educate ourselves. We've set up schools on tribal government and on our language and heritage. Our children must be our future leaders."

DONALD TIBBETTS

North Whitefield

OUT ON THE FARM, *when the snow gets crusted over and shiny, only a few withered stalks of grass and thicket break its surface. Chickadees seek bright red berries around the fence posts. The Belgian workhorse whinnies in the cold, his huge shaggy feet nervously pawing the ground.*

Donald Tibbetts banked the lower sides of the barn with hay, half hidden under condensed drifts. A warm orange light from bare bulbs sets the building apart from the darker folds of a moonless night. It is quiet except for the deep breathing of the cows and an occasional bovine moan. Their vapor mixes with the sharp smells of the barn.

Before dinner Tibbetts is weary and unshaven. He sweeps out the barn, unthinking; his gaze unfocused, his motions mechanical. Still, dairy farming has its satisfactions; Tibbetts wouldn't trade it for the world.

DONALD TIBBETTS / *North Whitefield*

"I WAS BORN HERE on a North Whitefield farm in 1920 to a family of four girls and three boys. My people are Maine-born as far back as the state and longer. When my father died at age 80, he was self-made and worth half a million dollars. Most of that worth was in the land.

"The land. That's what counts. I bought the land I own in 1946 for

[1 3 7]

$1,500 including the house and barn. Back then you could buy this place, some cows, and a horse for $10 an acre. Now you can't touch it. A farm like this is worth a minimum of $150,000. When you're fresh out of college, that's a lot of money.

"My wife and me, we're pretty self-sufficient. We've done alright with the land. Enough to raise six kids and live comfortably. Still, we're not as self-sufficient as my parents who only went to the store once a month. They had to be 'cause they couldn't get around much. There was just the mail carrier who would bring the newspapers out by horse on a wagon or sleigh with the mail. There was the old narrow-gauge railroad that ran up from Wiscasset to Sheepscot and Alna with freight and passengers. We used to ship our milk on it until it was discontinued in 1936. And there was private horses. Seems all the barns today are filled with cars.

"We never had many cars back then, although I did see one in the 1920's. Some doctor came out here in a Model-T Ford, and we all rushed out to see it. It had runners on the front and two sets of wheels which looked like bike tires. The roads were never plowed, so the car used to always get stuck, and a horse would have to be used to tow it out. Ayuh.

"We used to walk more. I walked to school in the morning and would call on one or two gals along the way. The school consisted of one room with all eight grades in it. It had a big pot-bellied stove near the teacher — one teacher. And we just learned the basics. Readin', writin', and 'rithmetic.

"People worked harder back then and didn't have the leisure we have now. There was no machinery to bring in the corn or hay, and most of the farmers like my father never had a vacation in their lives. Now some farmers get five weeks off!

"For fun we'd have skating parties. We'd go down to the pond after dark, build a big bonfire on the middle of it, sit down, and roast marshmallows and hotdogs. Skate. Sneak into a corner with a good lookin' girl on occasion. And skate some more.

"Another fun thing back in my father's time was barn raisin' and house-movin'. I liked hearin' about the house movin's since it sounded like one big party. You'd bring in three or four barrels of spiked apple cider, and everyone would bring their oxen. Then they'd jack up the building and roll it along on logs hitched behind all of the oxen in town. You could hold parties and dances sometimes in the houses while they were still jacked up and on the road. It was fun. And all those who came to help were called 'bees,' like worker bees in a hive. If someone was sick, a bee would come in to help out with cuttin' firewood or with chores. It was nice.

"Things were generally harder back in my father's time, just as the winters were worse. They used to have to shovel snow away from the first story windows all the time, and you just burned wood for your heat. Haulin' loads of firewood wasn't as easy then as it is today.

"Today, we get in my truck and haulin' is warm and effortless. Back then, we used to have to take a pair of horses and a set of sleds with old steel runners. I remember goin' into Gardiner with my father. The runners would be squeakin' on the snow, the moon was out, and it was cold. We covered ourselves with blankets to keep warm, but sometimes we'd have to get out and walk along beside to ease the load on the horses. Still those work horses, like mine today, love to haul and were happiest and warmest in front of a good load.

"We also used to cut ice on the Sheepscot and Kennebec Rivers. There was no mechanical refrigeration so you needed that ice and an ice house to keep it in the summer.

"Come January, I'd go to the river and mark off blocks of ice on the surface. We used ice saws which were about six feet long and had teeth that faced downwards. You sawed the ice with vertical motion against the tide so the blocks would float downriver away from you to a ramp. Then it would be loaded onto sleighs, and the horses would cart it off to the ice houses.

"We wore ice creepers which were cleats with four prongs that we strapped to our feet to keep from slippin'. There were no creepers for the horses; they slipped all the time. And if the horses slipped into the water or went through the ice — we would pull tight on a choke rope around their necks. For some reason, that makes them jump out to the surface to get air and has saved many a horse's life.

"After the ice was cut we'd go to the paper mills and collect sawdust to pack in around the ice blocks. In that way they wouldn't melt together in summer. The ice houses were insulated. Then we'd store our milk in the ice houses, and sell the ice to companies that shipped it by schooner all over the world.

"With farmin', you do different work in different seasons, so it doesn't ever get repetitive. Usually we'd start the day out by gettin' up early and buildin' a wood fire. Then we'd put the tea kettle on and go out to feed the cattle. By then it's time to feed yourself and drink your tea, and then you have to go out and milk the cows. Milk machines didn't come onto the scene

till 1938 so it took longer.

"One thing that hasn't changed at all is newspaper time. You do that after you milk the cows. Then you feed the hens, pigs, and dogs. The cats can fend for themselves, and lived out in the barn.

"We have also raised chickens and our own vegetables. The garden produce was for our own use, but we sold corn commercially. Corn was planted using a horse and a one-row corn planter machine which has a big wheel to pack the ground and two tubs on top. The tubs held corn seed and phosphate fertilizer, and they were deposited at regular intervals.

"We used no chemicals in the garden. No sir! But we had to pull all the weeds by hand. That took time and was a real backache. We still pull most of the weeds by hand to avoid usin' atrocene.

"And we grew hay. All of the mowin' was done by horse and hand. If we got one field of hay cut back then, it was a great day's work. Now we can cut half of a farm's worth of hay usin' a tractor — and bale it. Better than a scythe.

"Finally, there were the chores. There was plenty of barn and house maintenance to be done all of the time, firewood to be cut, and compost to spread. The chicken coops had to be fumigated once a year to prevent disease, and each spring we'd have to repair fence stakes from winter's frost heave damage.

"So that's basically the way life used to be on the farm, and in some ways how it's changed today. It's a life full of hard work, but did you ever smell that earth in spring? Boy, that makes it worth it all. I wouldn't move off the farm for anything!"

JOHN HEDMAN

New Sweden

Aroostook County is a vast, subterranean potato factory — a dull, starchy landscape that blossoms once a year in a splash of pink and white. Clouds roll across the sky casting blue shadows on the fields. The furrowed earth is dotted with barrels. Once filled, trucks cart the tubers into silos buried in the insulating earth. By winter the landscape turns sullen once again until the earth is covered by a fresh tarpaulin of snow.

John Hedman lives in New Sweden on a farm granted to his family under the 1860 Homestead Act. Like his father he succumbed to the gravitational pull of potato farming — a back-breaking, fingernail-caking business. Hedman describes the lure of tradition.

John Hedman / *New Sweden*

"My family came over from Sweden in the third wave of immigrants in 1871 on my father's side and in 1880 on my mother's. Maine was a frontier then, and these immigrants were brought over to homestead the land. Our farm passed from my great-grandfather down to my grandfather, father, and me. We have always been a self-sufficient operation with potatoes, cattle, sheep, pigs, berries, and a garden. We have a woodlot to round things out. This has continued for about 100 years now.

"The early pioneers were rugged individualists with an incredible work ethic. This ethic became ingrained in me from childhood on. Instead of hearing Mother Goose stories before bed, my father would tell us about grandpa Eric and the incredible things he did.

"Eric Hedman was born in 1864 and came over with his father on one of the early boats. His father died when he was 13, so he became the man on the farm at an early age. He pioneered this land until he died in 1954 at age 90.

"Grandpa was eccentric until the end. He was absent-minded. Although he was only five foot four inches tall, he had a habit of doing amazing things. Like clearing our land. He did it through trial and error — enduring disease, hardship, and isolation to make our lives easier.

"Our soil on this homestead is glacial, and there are a lot of boulders and stones that were dragged and left here. So it was up to my Grandpa to clear the land to prevent hidden rocks from breaking plow blades and so on.

"Well, the early settlers were all self-taught with dynamite and explosives which they used to blow out huge boulders. I don't know why most of them didn't kill themselves in the process of trial by error, but they didn't. And my grandfather was one of them. He took these two sticks of dynamite and dug a little hole under a boulder that he wanted to remove. Then he lit the fuse and ran away. Well, it didn't go off so he waited for what he thought was a reasonable amount of time and then figured that the fuse had just burned up. He walked back to the rock, leaned right down over it to see, and then . . . KABAAM!! Little pieces of rock just flew through the air and cut his face and clothes up. His eyes were filled with mud and pebbles, and he was blinded — temporarily. He was a quarter of a mile away from the house when the explosive went off and crawled home on his hands and knees, feeling along the farm road that he must have known literally like the back of his hand.

"The doctor's explanation of why he lived through it was that he was so close to the explosive that the real impact went right by him and hadn't yet built itself up to full velocity. Well, he didn't go right out farming the next day, of course, and he had slightly impaired vision afterwards, but he lived through it to blow up many more rocks — supposedly a little bit wiser for the experience.

"My grandfather liked to take a bit of snuff every now and then. One day he was up in the barn loft, throwing hay down to the cattle below. He was standing close to the edge of the loft, took some snuff, and sneezed. The

recoil sent him head over heels off the loft, and he fell three stories into the soft seat of an old sleigh beneath him! Now this is true and was verified by a lot of people.

"Once again he had to crawl home on all fours, badly bruised, but he again survived. My grandmother by this time was used to his being accident-prone and coming home that way, and probably wasn't too surprised.

"In addition to the myth of his being absent-minded and accident-prone was the recklessness of the man. It was often hard for us children to tell if Grandpa was really a brave and courageous man, or if he was a damn fool.

"One time he'd been cutting wood in back of the farm when he spotted some bobcat tracks. Well, he had this idea of the all-around man who could hunt, farm, trap, shoot, and fish, and he also knew that bobcat skins fetched a fair price. Grandpa didn't know anything about trapping, but felt he could certainly learn. So he set a trap by those tracks and did everything right . . . except he didn't anchor the trap. So he returned to find that he'd captured the bobcat one night, but that it had walked off, trap and all.

"Well, he started to follow the tracks, which must have looked a mite peculiar, and didn't go far before he found the cat up in a tree. He had his musket rifle with him, but being the man he was, forgot to bring the bullets. (Grandpa was always doing things like going fishing without bait, and holding dinner parties without food.)

"He figured that there had to be more than one way to skin a cat, and he had no fear. Even though a bobcat, especially a wounded one, is over 30 pounds of teeth and claws and can be mean, Grandpa decided to climb up the tree after him and poke him with the gun. 'It was just a cat, you know.'

"The cat, fortunately, just spit at him and slapped with his paw and wouldn't get out of that tree for anybody. Even Grandpa.

"So he climbed down the tree again and started to rip off his buttons from his vest. He put some powder in his gun, jammed down some buttons, and up and shot the cat. The impact of the buttons was enough to sting the cat, who jumped from the tree, and somehow my grandfather managed to kill it. The story goes on that the buttonless hunter returned home with buttons strewn all over the woods and everything flapping, but with a bobcat skin. And my grandmother chewed him out for ruining his vest.

"My grandfather was also a great outdoorsman who loved to walk. Upon the coming of school buses, he told us all to walk. And he used to be an auctioneer on Saturday afternoons. The auctions were held 15 miles away, and he'd go to town on cross-country skis. And after it was over he'd ski back 15 miles through the woods and fields in the moonlight.

"Grandfather lived through the Industrial Revolution and always had trouble with automation. He owned one of the first cars in New Sweden, and was very proud of that. He was also a show-off, bought the biggest and longest car he could find. For some reason or other he couldn't stand to be passed on the road. We would be coming home from church and one of the neighbors would go flying by. We wouldn't let Grandpa drive on Sundays, and he'd be in the back seat, bouncing up and down livid and yelling, 'CATCH HIM! What did you let him pass you for?!'

"Grandma would be sitting next to him and cry, 'Eric, for God's sake, who cares?!' He never gave any reason other than, 'Just don't ever let them pass you!'

"And when Grandpa was driving himself . . .

"He used to play games and slow down so the other guy behind him would tailgate. Then he'd speed up when he tried to overtake him. That was a great accomplishment.

"He was a terrible driver. He would be talking to you, and there would be people walking on the road. It got so that they saw him coming and would dive under the nearest bush to get away. He'd go off the road and onto the shoulder before he ever realized it and was then self-righteous in correcting you that he never scared anyone or even came close.

"And when we finally bought a tractor, he had trouble. The first time he got on it, he just went around in circles. We'd tell him, 'Turn the other way.' So he'd turn the steering wheel the other way and go in circles again. He's spend whole afternoons going around in circles and condemning modern machinery. You see, he was used to a horse. You pulled one way on the reins, and the horse turned and then automatically corrected itself. Not so with the tractor."

"My childhood memories of farming were not pleasant. I had mixed feelings. I liked the land and the fresh air, but I couldn't appreciate those things fully 'cause I had to work. And there were distasteful jobs that I had to do with mosquitoes flying around my head, and my father not being at all pleasant.

"Then there was the whole business of primogeniture where the oldest son inherits the farm. My older brother hated farming, and he must have hurt my father when he left. Not that father feels bad that I'm here in his place. At least I'm second in line. But I was very conscious of that.

"And then there was always a kind of pleading from my father to the tune of, 'Wouldn't you stick around?' At the time, I was 18 and wanted to go on to college. My father wouldn't have been at all disappointed if I didn't go but stayed right here and got into it. But my mother would have been displeased, and a big family argument would have started.

"After graduating from the University of Maine at Orono in English, I did return to take over the farm. Part of the reason was to continue being a part of the living myth which my grandfather had started. But also, my father quit the farm and left me a few beat up old pieces of machinery. I had traveled and had experienced a bit of city life, which I detested.

"I found that I was just as stubborn and individualistic as all the rest, even though I thought that I wouldn't make the same mistakes my father and others made, since I had a college education. I overestimated myself, but perhaps needed that kind of overestimation to get myself back into the farming scene. I may have been a little bit young, dumb, and stupid, but I wanted to do it *my* way and take my lumps — as well as the credit. The first year I pulled myself out of debt and got a few thousand dollars ahead. Then I got hooked into the farm syndrome.

"Now, you can't take the syndrome for granted! If you look at the frontier mentality, at least in the movies, drama, and dime novels, those settlers were gamblers. Everything you did when you picked up to settle a new, unknown area was a gamble. And that spirit has carried over into the Aroostook potato business that I'm in.

"Gambling and the business of taking risks is an American way of life. It gives you the feeling of being a cut above other people who are into, say, the nine to five routine. So the farmers who have wives and four kids to support continue to gamble.

"There is a certain mystique about being involved in a risky business, and that's why farmers frequently gloat when they've had a really good year. They have really accomplished something. They'll plant in the spring and put all of their savings into the crop, leaving just the bare necessities to get by with until harvest. We lived that way and stayed self-sufficient. We'd pick berries for dinner and get our milk from the cows and our vegetables from the garden. We lived frugally. That was part of the gamble.

"Many farmers turn into compulsive gamblers — sometimes out of necessity. They'll go and push their credit to the absolute limit. They'll lie to banks and collect $5,000 from every bank in the County. Then they'll ask for aid from the Farmer's Home Administration and all of the other government agencies. Somehow they manage to keep going and just become that much more gritty.

"You start to mend the kid's clothing and make the car go one more year. Then fortunately, every few years, they'll get a good harvest and knock off a few debts to keep up their credit so they can weather another series of bad years. So they're hooked into a vicious cycle.

"I've been hooked too. There's the mentality that just because of a few bad years, 'You *can't* quit. Don't *give* up!' Quitters here lose all of the community's respect so there's real pressure on you not to. Plus the mentality that maybe next year things will be good. So we're all hooked.

"I talk with non-farmers and say that I'm going to lose $4,000 this year and they can't understand it. They say I'm working one job at school to pay for another, which is true some years. But, after two good years, I can't get away from it, and defend farming like all of the old farmers I tried to be different from. So I'm making my father's mistakes which I thought I could avoid, and am caught up in a fatalistic farmers' historical dilemma. There is no escape, and no desire to escape.

"I farmed mostly on the side as a form of therapy. Most of the time I'm a school teacher. Working with kids some days is a pain, and you can get strung out. Working with an inanimate object like a potato is satisfying.

"Farming in so many ways is tangible. When you put in an acre of crops, you know exactly where you started and what you got done that day. You can sit back on your tractor and see what you've accomplished and say, 'This is good!' There's no other feeling like that.

"It's unlike teaching where there's a lot of abstracts and you're mostly dealing with concepts. There are a lot of concepts to farming too, of course, but they're more concrete.

"I can remember one spring when we still had cattle, and there was a good pile of manure out in the back of the barn. We were having negotiation problems at the school between the teachers and administrators and things were starting to get self-seeking and nasty. The whole atmosphere was unhealthy so I used to come home and just put on my shitkickers. I stood out there in 90-degree heat in the middle of that manure pile and spread it around with a shovel. And I was happy! That was my thing at the time, and it was therapeutic."

JENNIE CIRONE

South Addison

THERE is something luring and hypnotic about lighthouses, something romantic and charismatic, something that attracts artists and photographers, poets and daydreamers. Something special.

Maybe it's the surrounding sea, or their precarious perches on towering bluffs and tiny islands. Powerful lights seduce one's gaze and imagination, like moths entranced by the calling of the flames.

There were once lighthouse keepers, night watchmen of the sea. They would live in the houses by the lights. In doldrums, they would whitewash walls, shine lenses, and grease gears. They made certain that bells would toll and foghorns bellow. When the lights failed to warn away ships in fog or storm, keepers would risk their lives rowing out into the surf in sturdy dories. Marooned survivors were rescued, waterlogged bodies recovered from the rocks and kelp.

Some keepers valued the existential life of logkeeping and solitaire. Surrounded by ocean, they would travel to the distant reaches of their minds as currents of wind, wave, and cloud broke across the bows of their islands.

Other keepers were less stoic. They would stock their houses with food, staples, family, and friends. Jennie Cirone was the daughter of one such keeper on Nash Island.

Cirone remembers the storm that split the island into Little Nash and Big Nash. She remembers the terrible drama of shipwrecks and drownings — visiting death. She remembers the marvelous family intuition — a supersensory rapport with every gear, chain, and pulley of the lighthouse mechanism, its metallic heartbeat clanking in the night. There were chickens in the barn, a bull in the yard, and sheep on the knolls. Every two weeks the ferry came with mail and school teachers. For Cirone, formal education was catch-as-catch-can. Between lessons the teachers kept getting married to her brothers.

Keepers and their families are no longer on Nash, Pemaquid, Portland Head, Owl's Head, Matinicus, Monhegan, Manana, Southwest Harbor, Kittery, Quoddy Head, or Grand Manan. Machines do very-well-thank-you, and the Coast Guard has turned maintenance into an exact science. Still, Cirone's gaze is distracted past her house out to sea — toward a ghost. Luring and hypnotic, the light of Nash beckons to her.

JENNIE CIRONE / *South Addison*

"I WAS BORN IN MCKINLEY and lived with my parents, sister, and seven brothers on Nash Island for 18 years. It was great living on the island. We had barns, hen houses, and our house next to the lighthouse. There were no trees. To get to the water, we had to haul our peapods down the steep ways.

"I don't think we ever sat down to a meal where there wasn't anywhere from one to a dozen guests. All of my brothers and sister had their friends over and their families. Some stayed for months at a time. And their relatives from Portland came in the summer. The house was always full.

"For school there was one teacher who used to stay at all the islands for two weeks at a time. We had maybe four weeks of school all winter. The only problem was that just as soon as a teacher came over to stay with us and teach, one of the boys would marry her, and that would be the end of that. Four out of seven of my brothers married school teachers. It got so bad that they had to start sending us to school on the mainland. I hated it, and quit when I was 13. I got in a peapod and simply rowed back to Nash Island. I told my father that I would never go back, but wanted to go a-lobsterin'. So I did.

"I started haulin' traps when I was 10 years old. Nothin' to it really. Bait the traps with heads, put a pot in the water, mark it, and haul it up. My sister and father would go out in one boat one way around the island, and I would go in another boat the other way.

"I once got caught in a squall at age 13. The winds and chop was so rough that you could see air underneath lobster boats where the trough of the wave was. The whole keels were exposed. I kept wonderin' if my strength was goin' to hold up long enough for me to row ashore. And it was tricky rowin' into huge breakers. I'd have to time it and coast in between breakers. There were three big waves and then a fourth which flattened out. Then it would all repeat. I had just a split second to catch that fourth wave and coast into the slip. But I never missed. The same thing went on when I went out. We used peapods which were double-ended. When a sea came astern of it, it would lift unlike a square-sterned boat which would cause the wave to break into it.

"My father was a big, strong man, but he used to always get seasick. And mother. . . . The only thing I ever felt sorry about was when I headed in from a rough day of haulin' traps. A sou'wester blew up, and I was tired. When I got home, mother asked me to take her a-fishin'. I was tired from beltin' the wind all day, but she says, 'Nobody ever takes me fishing.'

"So I says, 'Get your gear on, and I will take you fishin'. But I warn you, we'll be takin' a chance in this wind!'

"Well, we got out there, and I didn't realize how scared she was in those waves. We got out over the breakers, and I took her out about a mile. By then she was beggin' me to take her back but I says, 'No, I'm takin' you fishin'.'

"I tied her up to a buoy and started to haul some traps. My mother never let go of the boat at all. 'I want to go home,' she says.

"Well, I finally took her home after tellin' her, 'When I tell you that you're takin' a chance, believe me next time!' She never asked me to go fishin' again, and that's bothered me all these years.

"I still go out lobsterin' every summer.

"Sometimes my sister and I were the only ones on the island. Normally we used to have to do lighthouse service like polishing the brass and cleaning the lens and light so they wouldn't tarnish every day. We had to put the light out at sunrise, and turn it on at sunset. It was a red light.

[155

"Then we had to wind up the bell. We cranked it up just as you would a clock, and then it would go by itself. It would tick and tick, and it had three prongs. Everytime a prong hit a lever, the bell would ring out. Every 30 seconds, BONG. My sister and me would cheat once in a while by taking out one of the prongs so she'd run a third longer. But mother lived in the room next to the bell, and she'd be tapping. She knew it the minute that bell stopped. They were used to it — it didn't keep them awake at nights.

"When I was little, I used to also have to scale off the paint from the light tower before putting on a new coat of whitewash. My father put me in a bolster chair and hoisted me up. He says, 'Okay, go ahead and start right in.'

"I was petrified up there and yells, 'My hands wouldn't let go!'

" 'Don't be foolish,' he says.

" 'I tell ya, my hands wouldn't let go!'

"Well, that was it. My father let go the rope and let me drop 10 feet down the side of the tower. I was about 16 years old. After that my hands *did* let go, and I went to work.

"We was always busy doin' something on the island. We either made toy boats, or sleds, or traps. Never a dull moment, really.

"I had a brother who was always gettin' me in a mess. He's always bettin' me things, and I'm foolish when it comes to bettin'. One time, we had just gotten a bow and some arrows. 'I bet you can't hit that window in the house,' he says.

"Well, I won the bet and broke the window. When I came to dinner that night, there was my plate turned over with a bow and arrow under it.

"Other times we'd have a calm spell and would go look for wood for the fire. There was enough driftwood on the island to burn for 20 years, so we'd take out the peapods and load 'em up. My mother used to use this driftwood and put creosol on it. We called it pitchpine hardwood. We used to make biscuits and popovers in the oven. One time we put some of this wood in. It got so hot that it broke the casin' and blew the oven door right off! Today, it's harder to find so much wood.

"We also used to go picking blueberries and gull's eggs. We'd collect hundreds of these eggs and then throw them at each other by the bushel basket. My brother, who was 10, threw gull's eggs at the pig till he squealed and was up to his knees in the stuff. That pig was fed on milk and eggs when he wasn't being bombarded. He got up to 520 pounds.

"We had all kinds of animals like rabbits, ducks, geese, and sheep. They was our playthings. The greatest plaything for my sister and me was a sheep. We'd haul coal from the boathouse by sheep sled. We'd harness them up the same as you would a horse. And the ram we had was so big that three of us would ride him bareback.

"My sister was always gettin' into messes too. One day she decided to hook up the bull to the cart. So she hitched this big fella up, and everything was alright until the cart started to rub up against the bull's hind legs. That bull started to bellow and run from the cart, but my sister hung right on. The cow by this time heard the distressed bull and jumped the fence to come to his rescue. The only thing that stopped him, and saved my sister's life, was that the bull ran right into the boathouse wall. His horn became embedded, and he couldn't continue on through, which he would have, with my sister.

'I left the island at age 21 in 1933. I came to the mainland. We had bought an old car to use to go to the movies and the circus with. It was an old 1918 hot-mobile we got for about $9. My brother and his wife and me and my sister would go to the movies in it in the summer. We'd take a boat over and start out real early after haulin' traps. We had to start early to go to the movies 'cause the car would always break down, and get as many as 10 flat tires. These were the thin bicycle-like tires, and we couldn't get new ones so easy.

"The routine was that a tire would be punctured, and my brother would get out and light a fire to keep the mosquitoes away. Then I would blow the tire up and patch it. Sometimes we had to put on 10 patches on the way to Milbridge. Half an hour per patch. We'd get back from the movies just in time for the next day's lobsterin'.

"Sheep have always been my favorites. We had them on the island before I came over. One February we had a huge storm. The wind was so great, it shook some of the pictures off the wall. The big tree on the island was up-rooted and washed out across the sand bar. It separated the bar and since then, our island consists of Big Nash and Little Nash. So the cattle and sheep have to swim across from one to the other.

"Sheep don't like to swim, but they will if they have to. It's alright if they don't have too much wool on. If they're heavy with wool, they'll sink right down and drown. You can tell they're in trouble when they start to swim in circles. You have to get to 'em fast, or it's all over.

"We had four islands and kept as many as 300 sheep on them. Let's see. There was Nash's Island, Pond Island, Jordan's Delight, and Flat Island. And we knew all the sheep by name and character.

"Now, there's Carmen, Silky, Virginia, Ester, Perfect, Gurty, Aunt Jemima, Velvet, and Hurricane Tim for example. Hurricane Tim we named after my nephew's son who was born in a hurricane. And then there was Disaster who was found under a snow drift on one of the islands.

"In winter when we have big blizzards, sometimes the sheep are covered over with snow. All you see is a little bank. The whole island looks deserted. And if you go over to one of these banks and dig around it, you'll find them all huddled together in a self-made cave. They sleep that way. This year some were under snow from the 24th of December till the 16th of January. And Disaster had a bar of ice across her back and couldn't get up. I found her, took her home, and saved her.

"Spring is the worst time of the year for sheep. On our island, there's so many sheep grazing that they form foot paths and knolls. The frost kills the grass on top, but down below in the knoll it's all green.

"When sheep feed in the knolls, they'll stretch out to get some sun and roll over. If they fall on their backs with their feet stickin' up in the air, they're helpless. It's my job to put them right-side-up again.

"In the last five years, we've almost been ruined by eagles and black-back seagulls. It's against the law for the fishermen to feed the birds. They've been starving. There are recorded instances of gulls attacking fishermen for bait, clam, worms, and herring. They've come in as far as 15 miles to eat our blueberries.

"These black-back gulls will watch our lambs and wait for one to fall over on its back. There's usually one gull who sees this. He lets out a squawking sound, and then the whole flock comes down. They attack the lamb and eat it alive.

"These gulls start in by cutting off the lamb's tail. Then they peel the hide over its head like you'd peel a sock off from your foot. There wouldn't be a hole in the hide when they're finished — just hide and bones. It's horrible."

DANIEL BATES

Manana Island

No man is an island.

— JOHN DONNE

MAINE *is a land of narrow peninsulas and wide expanses of hills and forest. People go north to escape the tyranny of urban America with its industrial blight and sterile suburbs. Yet there is a breed apart for whom any place sewed onto the mainland isn't far enough. Island people.*

Island people can be found scattered about in the bays of Casco, Fundy, and Penobscot, and in tiny cabins in Somes Channel and the Gulf of Maine. There are enough saline islands off Maine's rocks to accommodate everyone from the most atonal misanthropes to those who value silence and surf, the cries of gulls, and the unhurried Order of the Universe. All kinds of people; all kinds of islands.

One of Maine's best known islanders was Captain Ray Phillips, the "Hermit of Monhegan." Formerly in the meat-packing business, he left the island of Manhattan in the 1930's when the quality of life became too spare. He bought a sailboat, charted a course for Maine, and landed on Monhegan.

Monhegan is a pastoral island that has claimed five-by-one-miles of ocean off Port Clyde. It is a place where freckled children play in the grass, where artists capture the light, where lobster boats circle buoys beneath towering cliffs. The sun-bleached ribs of foundered ships are sucked down by its sand. Deer amble through its sedge. Rosehips

grow along its white picket fences. There are stands of spruce so thick that one old man lost his direction in them. He starved to death leaving his bones to be recovered years later. When the fog rolls in, it softens the island like an Oriental watercolor, stranding its inhabitants in splendid isolation.

Yet Monhegan wasn't isolated enough for Ray Phillips. He chose to live 500 yards further on an islet in the harbor called Manana. There he built a ramshackle house from his dismembered sailboat, driftwood, and old U.S. Coast Guard crates.

Whether visionary or reactionary, Phillips was certainly misunderstood. Neither a hermit, nor of Monhegan, he was simply a gentle shepherd living by himself on an island in the harbor. He drank goat milk, poached occasional lobsters, and mowed hay with a scythe for cash. He scribbled notes on his walls, talked philosophy to himself, and played a mediocre game of chess. People called him "Captain" out of some dim association with his veteran past.

Phillips wore his hair long. His bulky, ill-fitting clothes smelled of sheep. Indeed, toward the end of his life, his sheep lived with him in the house.

Although Phillips died alone in 1975, there was irony in the gentle shepherd's life. Through isolation, he achieved unanticipated celebrity.

When Phillips died, Danny Bates took over his house. They had been friends and shared an interest in sheep. Bates and his family subsisted by raising chickens, vegetables, and goats whose milk was sold to Monhegan islanders under the trade name "Barbarian Cheeseworks." Like Phillips, Bates is an island person.

DANNY BATES / *Manana*

"**R**ay Phillips was born in 1897. He was a meat packer from New York City. He decided to get out of the meat-packing scene in the 1930's. He bought a sloop which he took around the Maine islands, found Monhegan, and camped there for a while. Then he bought some land on Manana for about $75. He built the house I'm in now and added some sheep.

"Ray was probably ahead of his time in a lot of ways. People thought he was really strange. They didn't understand why he had long hair which was exceptional in the 1930's. They didn't understand why he chose to live in a simple shack on Burnt Head. And they didn't understand why he left the money-making scene to chart out a new life. Still, he was friendly enough.

Nobody could find anything they couldn't handle about him, except maybe the smell of sheep.

"When Ray got to Manana, he started to build his house in sections, working his way up the hill and rocks from the sea. First he built a slip to pull his boat up out of the water on. Then he started on the barn, stoving up his sloop. It had a low curved roof — that had been the deck. Cleats were on it everywhere. Some of the spars and booms were used as beams for support. It was really beautiful and is where my garden is now.

"He also built the little square part of the house we're sitting in now as his living quarters. For materials, he'd use driftwood, and stuff salvaged from across the way. He also used packing crates he got from the Coast Guard station on the island. You can still see the stenciled 'U.S. COAST GUARD' on some of the walls here, which is neat. He also used shingles that people donated as well as windows.

"We can't say Ray knew much about foundations. He built this place on posts dug into the rock. Since everything is on a hill, there was a space underneath the floor. His sheep often stayed under there, and the manure built up around the posts and dissolved them. So we're sitting on posts rotted down to toothpicks. When the wind blows, you really know it. Especially in a nor'easter.

"We also have a brook running under our house which makes our goat pen a real mess. It's not too great. For one thing, a goat pen is supposed to be dry and clean. If we lived down there, and the animals lived up here in the house, then maybe it would be better. We could have a bubbling brook in our living room and trees. But as it is now, it's just a swamp down there.

"Between this house and the barn is a chicken coop that he built. And there's a workshop extension and a kitchen that we built, and a bedroom. We're just now starting to put sod on the roof here. I like the idea of an earthen roof.

"Ray kept adding on to the house since he needed a project to do to keep him busy here on the island. And he also moved rocks. Most of the piles of rocks you see around here he moved. I think it's a form of saying, 'I've been here,' and of making a monument to yourself. It's also a form of unconscious art. Any time you build a bridge or manipulate nature in some way, you're sort of making this kind of statement.

"Ray was funny. I don't know where he got his clothes, but he didn't make his own. And he used to wear two pairs of pants which were too big

[1 6 3

for him. There'd be a belt on the inner pair and a belt on the outer pair, and it was really bizarre to see. He probably slept in one pair and put the other pair on in the morning. He wore baggy, wool mittens.

"He was a little bit of a Holy Man around here. It wasn't that he was religious, but he had quite a library of philosophy and a lot of *Reader's Digests* which somebody must have donated to him. I don't think he would have subscribed himself. He would read a lot and scribble passages from the books all over the walls.

"He didn't do a whole lot of anything, but he did do a lot of thinking. This was unlike most people who are always doing a lot of things to keep themselves from thinking about their own mortality.

"He'd collect a lot of things, and when spring cleaning came around every few years, a lot of the stuff would go into the ocean.

"He kept sheep, probably because they're the animal that requires the least amount of upkeep. They need almost no attention, and they're interesting. He was very fond of them as company and would talk to them and himself I suppose. I talk to myself so I assume everybody does.

"Ray wasn't really a hermit. He had plenty of time and loved to talk to people. I think living alone had a lot to do with that. The less you're around people, the more you enjoy the exchanges. We find that's true here ourselves, especially in the dead of winter. He'd give people a whole afternoon when they came out. Like my grandmother who summered across the way on Monhegan. She was very rich and worldly, and thought it would be civic-minded of her to go out to the hermit and play chess with him. So she did.

"Ray also wrote letters to people, and they'd write back, which was cool. He had a few bureau drawers full of correspondence when we got here. We returned them to his sister. He had a few transistor radios and listened to them often, and occasionally he'd go into Rockland to get a shave and a haircut and to visit his relatives by Greyhound bus. But he didn't do that every year.

"When Ray was 60, he was thinking about getting a lady here! He decided to get a few things together before making proposals. He still didn't know who the lady was going to be, of course. He used his social security and veteran's benefits to buy matching plumbing fixtures, a bathtub, a toilet, and a sink. They were all brand new and of white enamel, and he built a ramshackle addition to the place so he could house the stuff. He even had curtains although there was no one to see here on the island. The only thing he didn't have was running water.

"Actually, he had hooked up a water system out of pieces of salvaged drain pipes and gutters which came down from the top of the hill on the island through the rock piles to the house. The water was carried on to a low roof and into a storage tank inside so he could fill a tub of water if he wanted to. But from the smell of Ray, nobody knows if he ever used it or not.

"And as for the tub and sink, he never carried through with finding a lady. The only ones to use the stuff were the sheep who filled them with manure.

"Ray was in his 70's when he got cancer of the throat. The last winter, he was really sick and knew it. He started to tell people on Monhegan that he wasn't gonna last 'til spring.

"It was really sad the way he went. He was eating baby food out of jars, and he couldn't keep the place up. The animals started living with him in the house. When we moved in after his death, we found several sheep heads on the floor, a sheep body in the closet which had been there way too long, and we had to clean out up to three inches of manure from off the floors. Ray died completely alone in 1975. He sort of wanted to let it happen, so I didn't offer to help. It would have been intruding in a way.

"When Ray died, people on Monhegan felt I was a natural shoo-in to take his place. My association with Ray, my goat, and my attitude sort of made me into a character in the eyes of the more conservative people living on Monhegan. I kind of enjoyed that, and started to develop my character.

"I had come from Lewiston to Monhegan around age 22. I bought a goat which I took with me wherever I went. That's how I met Ray — I brought it to Manana, and we talked about raising them. I used to wear a black cape and black sunglasses too. That was part of my 'character.'

"I was kind of cracking up inshore and got to thinking that Manana would be the ideal place to finish it up.

"I also started thinking just how beautiful Manana was, and that the poor hermit was sick and soon going to die. When he finally did die, people started joking, 'Hey Danny, when are you gonna move in?'

"Well, as it turns out, I did move in. I was about 23, and Amy was about 16. Amy summered on Monhegan, and I got a crush on her and seduced her — with a frisbee. We thought about it and went across the harbor.

"We support ourselves here by raising goats and selling cheese and milk under our brand, 'Barbarian Cheeseworks.' We raise our black and red flag out on our flagpole and sell to the store on Monhegan, and to other markets in Maine. We have a garden and grow some of our food, and I prop goat's heads on the fence posts to keep the heebie-jeebies away. They're everywhere so you've got to be careful. I also do some underwater work for the lobster-men on the boats, and sculpt.

"I don't get along with other people for any length of time. Often I think I'd like to have other people living here on the island, but then remember that even when you get two people together, immediately there's politics and complications.

"It's bad enough having to share this island with a Coast Guard Station and a fog horn and a glacial rock reputed by tourist brochures to contain Phoenician ruins without having other people around. And since we're only about 100 yards across from Monhegan, everybody can see what we're doing — and they watch. We welcome the fog when it rolls in. That way, we're enveloped and can do whatever we want without being seen.

"One thing that irritates us is when we're referred to as the new 'hermits.' The term hermit wasn't really applicable to Ray, and it isn't really applicable to us."

ALEXANDER *and*

KEITH LARRABEE

Stonington

STONINGTON *rests on a foundation of granite across from Isle au Haut. Many of its people were born in stark wooden houses with granite doorsteps, window sills, and door frames. When they die granite will mark their graves.*

The Larrabee brothers have stone dust in their blood. Alexander spent his life quarrying on Crotch Island before retiring, a broken man with a wheezing cough and rotten lungs. Keith revitalized the business in Stonington.

Where Alex is lean and gentle, Keith is rotund and blunt. His massive forearms and gut absorb the shock of jackhammers; he is oblivious to the violent repercussions of dynamite blasts in his quarry. Keith balances the abrasive business of quarrying with the soft touch of stone-masonry. He delicately carves monuments and engraves epitaphs. His work is timeless, like Stonington.

ALEXANDER LARRABEE / *Stonington*

"I WAS BORN IN STONINGTON IN 1916 to a stonecutting family. Three out of five brothers followed my father into the craft. I started working across the harbor on Crotch Island in the 1930's after apprenticing for a stonecutter.

[169

I learned to read stonecutting diagrams and to cut stone.

"It was all hard work. We got up around 5:00 A.M., had breakfast, and then everybody filed down to the docks to catch the company ferryboat by 6:30 A.M. The whistles would sound, and 200 men would start working. The sounds of pneumatic air compressors, dynamite, and jackhammers would continue from morning until the whistle blew again at 4:00 P.M. It was steady noise and pounding all day with dust in your eyes and lungs. We never wore masks to protect our breathing. By the end of the day your blood vessels were shot, your ears ringing, and your nerves was pounded to hell from the jackhammers. There were a fair number of accidents too. I've seen men get stoved-up and blasted away by dynamite. Still, work was scarce, and them men was glad to have a job.

"There were no benefits in those years. I made $2 a day at the start. When I retired in 1964, I was making $110 a week.

"That granite hill on Crotch Island was pretty high when we started. We whittled it down over 100 feet. We cut a tunnel through 40 feet of stone so that a cutter could walk in and cut the stone out. In winters it was so cold that they had to dynamite the ice in the channel so the barges could get through to tow out the granite. All freight and supplies came by boat to Deer Isle.

"They used big sawmills to cut the stone. The saws had steel blades and could cut the stone pretty fast. Then a big derrick crane would hoist these large blocks down to the barges and on to railroad cars that we had after World War II.

"Things winded down at Crotch Island due to competition from other granite quarries in Quincy, Massachusetts and Quechee Gorge, Vermont. There was also competition from the steel and concrete industries — that's what delivered the final blow. But I think that stone will come back as it becomes more economical.

"Granite from here was used for paving stones in Manhattan, window sills, subway tunnels, and Manhattan sewers, foundations, piers, and bridges. The New York City courthouse and Federal Building was made from Stonington granite as was the Triborough and George Washington bridge foundations and the Kennedy Memorial in Arlington Cemetery. It's beautiful to work with, and it lasts forever."

ALEXANDER *and* KEITH LARRABEE

KEITH LARRABEE

"I'M THE YOUNGEST OF THE LARRABEE BROTHERS and was born in 1928. Like Alex, I left school at an early age to go into the quarries. Now I have a little sawmill and make lobster traps on the side. I also carve monuments, but my real interest is quarrying.

"I don't see my starting up a new quarry here in Stonington as an effort to preserve a dyin' art or anything romantic like that. I'm in it for the money. The price of concrete and steel is going up, and granite's going to come back.

"I paid $5,000 for some land and got a loan on some bulldozers and drills. I plan to make this into a lucrative business. Take that 20-foot-long, four-foot-high pillar of granite we blew out today. That sells for about $300. Some days we make as much as $4,000. You can get wealthy.

"Everyday I stand on land that was never stood on by man before. That doesn't excite me.

"Granite is old. It was glacial. The stone comes up with layers of dirt in between it. It has been sectioned by the Earth's cooling a billion years ago. The sheet of granite we're standing on now may go down five feet to a seam or crack. The next layer of stone may go down 10 feet. Then more dirt. And so on. I run a test rod down to see how deep the seams are before we decide to quarry it out.

"In mining granite, we bulldoze the surface dirt and trees away. Once the rock is exposed, you look for hitters which are seams in the stone. Then you drill a small hole, put in your powder and dynamite along the seam, and blow out a block of rock. Blasting is an art in itself — you've got to know what you're doing.

"Once the stone is out, you drill holes along it and hammer wedges in. This forces a crack through the stone. A tap of the hammer will then split the stone in two. Then you load it on trucks, and off it goes to market.

"Stonecutting is a beautiful trade which I love. Some cutters today are as good with granite as Michelangelo was good with soft marble. Still, I wouldn't pay a quarter to see Michelangelo's art. I'd rather do than look.

"Stone masons date back to ancient Egypt. They shape the granite once

it's been quarried. Most like me pack a half gallon of whiskey before setting to work. It relaxes the mind — granite is forever and so are your mistakes. You want steady hands before you start cutting.

"You cut stone by following a blueprint. If it's a building, every section is diagrammed out. Then every stone is diagrammed into shape. Then you set to work with hammers, chisels, and lathes, cutting the stone with the grain. Finally, you polish the stone and set your pieces in place like fitting together a puzzle.

"I carve grave monuments on the side and sculpture stone Madonnas for graves using a mold. I make me a stencil for words to be engraved, and then set to work with the blueprint, lining up words by eye. I sandblast it, polish it, and sell it. They sell for $400 each, and I can do four a day. It's good work, and I love it."

DAHLOV IPCAR

Robinhood

IMAGINE *a two-dimensional world where regal gazelles leap and play in a geometric jungle with exotic parrots, butterflies, cheetahs, and zebras. Imagine a world suffused with sunbeams. Imagine a world where feudal knights come to life on a chessboard and joust for Ladies. Imagine the world of Dahlov Ipcar.*

Born in 1917, Ipcar is the daughter of William and Marguerite Zorach. Influenced by her father's sculpture and her mother's painting, she shunned formal art training. "I became my own school of art."

Ipcar writes and illustrates children's books, and paints in the sun-filled studio of her Georgetown house, built in the Franklin stove era. Each day she attends to various projects set up on easels in different corners of the room. She'll stare at the canvasses, day-dreaming designs and mosaic patterns. Underlying forms and moods emerge from the deep recesses of her mind, taking on lives of their own as they come to light.

"I never know how something is going to turn out," she says nervously. A jovial crack is in her voice. "Often it's a pleasant surprise."

DAHLOV IPCAR / *Robinhood*

"Animals are so beautiful to me. I never outgrew them as a child. I have managed to keep my childhood perceptions of them from trips to the

Museum of Natural History, the Bronx Zoo, and movies. I used to go to Simpson's Animal Farm on the Old Bath Road to look at the animals. Over the years I've gotten a feeling for what wild African animals look like. I have internalized their movements and personalities. I am quite detached from Maine when I paint. I need never leave my house in Georgetown to create. Art is like that for me.

"I stylize my work, simplifying animals into their underlying forms. I feel that I can't accurately reproduce the spring landscape outside my picture window here literally. It must first go through my mind, and then be transformed into form and feeling. I paint that.

"Forms come closest to a visual language of beautiful abstract shapes. I can't explain this language, but intuitively I'm oriented towards it. I like to combine abstract work with real images as opposed to pure Norman Rockwell social realism or pure abstracts like minimalism. I enjoy patterns and design.

"In a mural I painted for a bank in the Auburn Mall, I used two-thirds-lifesize animals in a non-intellectual cubist style. I used geometric forms to remove depth from paintings. Trees became triangles; sunbeams became horizontal forms. On a single plane you don't crowd the animals. You depict different times and places all on the same dimensional surface.

"Ideas will just hit me all at once. I wake up some mornings with a pattern in my mind. Man is a pattern making animal, a visual animal, I think.

"When I was young I once had a fever and measles. I remember lying on my back in bed, looking up at the ceiling. I saw these rabbits running upside down so I turned on my side, and they ran sideways. I turned on my stomach to get them running right-side-up along the bedroom floor.

"It was like the dream images you see at night, like seeing a Mexican fiesta in my pillow, or 100 snakes slithering down a forest of trees, or 100 flowers and patterns on the bedpost. It's hard to hold on to these dream images, but sometimes I do get ideas from them. Early morning is a creative time of day for me.

"I've painted a design of fish in the sea and a grand master chess game that I thought up after reading *Alice In Wonderland* — the annotated edition. The actual *Alice* was a chess phantasmagoria. It didn't follow the rules of chess at all. Carroll must have been a very poor player.

"I also make soft sculptures with cotton fabrics built around wire armatures. I stuff these with malleable kapok, an oriental material. I have hanging in my studio a kapok pig, a fawn, and a horse. I also painted Saint George and

the Dragon, and Lady Godiva sitting on a tiger. It's all a part of my twilight world.

"When I write and illustrate children's books, I like to keep things straightforward and realistic. Getting away from the story line can be confusing. I don't like my illustrations to be merely decorative. I like to teach concepts like how to count, or morals.

"In my book, *The Cat of the Night*, I depicted what I thought a cat might see through its eyes. Mostly silhouettes. The idea was for children to relate to the shapes, to turn outlines into real-life objects. It was a lesson in shape recognition. I had a heck of a time trying to convince the book's editors that it was about more than a cat going out for a simple walk.

"I enjoy the challenge of fitting animals into a puzzle. Sometimes my husband Adolph and I see deer, foxes, and birds on the farm. But I no longer need them to paint. I have memorized entire zoos in my head. I draw upon this memory and bring it to life in my paintings."

ROSA LANE

Orland

Maine *is not all blueberries and sunshine. Some people live in a twilight netherworld of depressing downtown bus stops, run-down bars, and tacky billiard halls. There are tar-paper shacks that collect filth, rats, and stagnant water along with the stench of open sewage. There are impoverished, broken families, ragged children, and chronically un-employed people. There are disease, malnutrition, illiteracy, and spirals of despair. Hidden from tourists and the Chamber of Commerce, despair seethes just below the sur-face — out of sight, out of mind. There is in Maine, what Robert Coles calls a "culture of poverty."*

"I guess I was an oddball kid," Rosa Lane said, "but I just knew there was something else to life than marriage and the raise-your-kids pay-the-rent rut. I didn't want to live and die in New Harbor after an honest and hard life. Secretly, I saved up all my money from picking strawberries and other odd jobs until I was 18. Then I got out."

Lane left New Harbor to work her way through Wilmington College in Ohio. "It was there that I saw my first Afro," she said. "I marched against the Vietnam War. I demonstrated against the Kent State killings. I alienated myself from my parents. After school I did what I never anticipated doing. I hitchhiked back to Maine. Not to see my parents, but to dig clams in Bristol and decide what I wanted to do with my life."

Lane saw an advertisement in the Maine Times which landed her a job as a teacher in the Hancock County Headstart program. She worked there with disadvantaged children for three years and with Homeworker's Organized for More Employment (H.O.M.E.). She taught the poor and chronically unemployed to read and write, to farm, *and to fashion saleable crafts. She tried to break people out of the rut of rural poverty.*

Lane also worked on the night shift of the Saint Regis paper mill in Bucksport. She earned enough money to build her own house. At night she shared poetry with a women's study group and challenged the traditional role of women. "I worked out a guilt trip for having grown up in poverty," she said. "I questioned traditions."

R O S A L A N E / *Orland*

"IN MAINE HISTORY, 60 years ago, most of the state was self-sufficient farms and fishermen. There were clam diggers, potato farmers, sheep raisers, and lobstermen. They were self-employed 'cause it never occurred to them to do things any differently. Industrialization hit Maine years later than the rest of the nation, and in some places, not at all.

"There is a psychological breakdown that occurs when self-sufficient people turn to industry. People move from healthy rural areas into the cities. The land gets broken up and developed. Psychological poverty sets in, a poverty of the mind. Like my work at the Saint Regis paper mill. It was routine, degrading, impersonal work. Not at all satisfying aside from making a living.

"My father barely hung on with the skin of his teeth as a lobster fisherman. He kept at it because of an intuitive fear that if it fell through, he'd have to go to work *for* somebody. It was that old Republican do-it-yourself individualism that gripped him. And the fear of spiritual poverty should he have to work for someone else on some assembly line.

"I could see three worlds. One world contained people I worked with who were in poverty. As a girl I had watched my family work their way out of this world. It is a world of apathy where people have a stove, but freeze because they can't seem to get it together to go out and split the wood.

"I became engulfed seven days a week working with people at Headstart and H.O.M.E. I began to realize that many of these people had a different set of values. They were not unhappy in their world of poverty. One family used to literally crawl into a big bed and hibernate through the winter, happy as clams in a shell. It was discouraging trying to throw a monkey wrench into the cycle of poverty.

"It was then that I realized that poverty was defined as an economic plight, and all solutions were idealistic. This way of thinking ignored the psychological poverty that was at the root of apathy and economics. Poverty is a spiritual condition.

"To combat this poverty, I designed an agricultural program at H.O.M.E. where I didn't give anything to anyone for nothing. No alms. I designed contracts. If I gave people two goats, they had to give back offspring. We grew from managing 12 farms to 66 farms. Many people were involved and broke out of their apathy. But it was interesting that they chose to stay out of the factories. They remained on the land, working the farms.

"The second world was recognizing that material wealth and the economics of poverty was an idealistic way of tackling the problem. It was a superficial way of looking at the problem that offered no lasting solutions.

"The third world for me was an attempt to deal with my own discouragement. I was getting sick of finding dead and decaying rats lying on people's kitchen floors. I was figuratively bringing those rats and my social work home with me. I was succumbing to my parents' workaholic work ethic. After a while I developed a safety valve. After work I learned to tell people in my mind to keep their poverty — I didn't want it. And then I began to search for a creative outlet.

"I turned to poetry. It went from a fun-loving hobby to a terrifying obsession. I have no choice now but to follow the poet's path. It's like staring into a bright light. If you stare too long you feel its draw pulling you in. At that point you're on the edge of yourself. There's that danger of falling off into your subconscious, and that's terrifying.

"At the pre-poem stage something just emerges up in the form of disconnected images. As your hand moves and writes, it's like you're given a riddle that you must solve. You've got to bring the riddle together, find a tone and its message. Like a sculptor, you've got to free imprisoned images out from the wood.

"Poetry images are like butterflies flying around your head. If you don't have a net to catch them, they're gone. I'll be driving along, and these images and moods will spring out at me. I keep a pencil and paper handy to keep from losing them.

"Poets are the readers of living symbols. Sometimes I just can't read. Either something hits me too strongly, or I'm just not receiving. I have to internalize the outer world. I look at a stove. I bring in the image of that stove and reflect it on my retina. The stove is still on the floor, but it's also inside me. Then I have to personally interpret the stove into my own thoughts and language. You also develop an ear for rhythm.

"The eye and ear are just two organs of perception. In poetry there are lots of organs of perception — not necessarily sensual. You've got to use these perceptions to tackle images and themes. This sort of perception is what also gives you insight into that world of poverty."

SCOTT *and*

HELEN NEARING

Harborside

SCOTT AND HELEN NEARING *left Manhattan to pioneer a homestead when most people were migrating back to the cities. They hand-built their home in Vermont from stone, grew their own vegetables, heated their rooms with wood, and produced maple products as a cash crop. In 1954 they moved to Harborside, Maine, on Cape Rosier, and built Forest Farm, their present homestead.*

"Our lifestyle was obvious to us at the time," Helen said. "We would never have written about it in Living the Good Life *if Pearl Buck hadn't suggested to us that it wasn't obvious to a lot of other people."*

Since the book was published hundreds of people have pilgrimaged to the Nearings. They come to learn about organic farming in solar greenhouses, to help split wood, to farm the land, to sit by the sea listening to the tranquil calls of white-throated sparrows, to share song and philosophy. All find two hardworking, unpretentious people who dress in dungarees and workshirts, their shoes heavy, their palms callused.

Helen was born in 1904. She goes about her business with the confident swagger of a woman half her age. Her gray hair is short-cropped, like her speech. She is mentally impatient and physically agile, filling every moment with the chores of gardening, canning, cooking, and writing. There is always a soup cooking on her stove. She has become maternal towards "Scotto," her husband.

Born in 1883, Scott lives out his philosophy of physical hand labor and intellectual radicalism. He rises with the sun to chop wood, haul water, think his thoughts. His

shoulders bunch and his head droops with the burden of a century. The good life out-
doors has crevassed his face with a thousand wrinkles. Blue eyes shine from the folds with
compassionate intensity. He sets an example of health by his own longevity.

Scott ran for mayor on the Socialist Party ticket against Fiorello La Guardia in the
1930's. Still in the public eye in the 1980's, he appeared as a real-life witness to the
Russian Revolution in Warren Beatty's Reds. *"I never saw the movie," he rasps. "Too*
long to sit through."

SCOTT AND HELEN NEARING / *Harborside*

"SCOTT AND I have great spiritual resources," Helen says. She is suffused with ocean light in the living room overlooking Penobscot Bay. As she
speaks her eyes and nimble hands never leave the knit-one-purl-two of a
sweater she knits.

"For us life is stimulating from simple things: breathing fresh air deeply,
weeding, sunshine. The things that made Thoreau's life so rich. People in
Thoreau's time thought his life was empty. All he did was plant beans, take
endless walks around Walden Pond and Concord, and enjoy the people he
met along the way. People didn't understand us either for years for doing the
same sorts of things. They flocked to New York for outside stimulation."

"Thoreau wasn't sophisticated enough, perhaps?" I ask. "The word troubles
me. What do you think of sophistication, Scott?"

"I stay away from it."

Helen reaches into the bookcase behind her and pulls out *Webster's*
Dictionary. "Sophisticated," she says. Her voice is guttural, her look pure
concentration. "Sophist is a man of wisdom. Worldly. 'Sophisticated: a lack
of simplicity or naturalness refined to the point of artificiality.... worldly.'

"We've travelled all over the world, but we remain simple. I wanted to
call my cookbook *Simple Food for Simple People.* The publisher wouldn't have
it. It was titled *Simple Food for the Good Life.* Somehow the word 'simple' has
become an insult to our society. We're out of step by living a natural life out
here in the sticks. Still, we think that it's often the people living in the cities
who are unnatural and artificial.

"It boils down to those inner resources again. Most people who have accepted the nine-to-five humdrum life of the slave pen never had any. Or they try to regain them on weekends and vacations.

"Losing those resources starts early. I recall one young son of a wealthy family. He had all the best toys and television. He grew up with all of these outer distractions. Without them, he was lost. Bored. Unable to play on his own. That was the start of his losing inner resources. Scott and I, on the other hand, may be alone with ourselves but we're never lonely. We have a life full of joy and surprise. I have my music and years of thoughts, memories, and memorized poetry to keep me company. Should I ever be thrown in jail, and it could happen if the government changes over as it did in Nazi Germany, I pray that I get a solitary cell as opposed to a cell full of gabby women. A paucity of outside stimulus engenders inner resources. We have them."

"How about Maine?" I ask.

"In the mountains of Vermont, people were provincial," Helen says. "They had always stayed in the mountain valleys. They were ingrown in their ways and highly suspicious of newcomers, including us. At times they were intolerant. Our friendly gestures were met with suspicion, even when we gave away our land when we moved.

"Here, I offered some maple sugar we made to Alice Gray down the road. She accepted it gratefully. She didn't question my motives, and we've been friends ever since. It's like that with most people in Maine. I think it's our proximity to the sea. People are less insular. They're better travelled and more tolerant. There is something therapeutic about the salt air, too."

I ask Scott why he left Manhattan so long ago.

"When you go into a building, you often see a sign on the wall reading, 'This hall is safe for occupation by 250 people,'" he says. "If you try to put 2,500 people in the room, the floor might cave in. You're foolish to bring in more people 'cause you endanger the lives of the room's occupants. Yet they do this in Manhattan. That's what's wrong.

"Regulation is needed for a group of people to get maximum satisfaction out of the life they're living, individually and collectively. But to regulate Manhattan, there'd have to be a revolution first. A whole new set of conditions and basic propositions. In the Mexican Constitution of 1917, there is a very interesting phrase, 'The natural resources of Mexico are the property of the people of Mexico.' It should be so for New York."

"What do you include under 'natural resources?'"

"In New York City, it would be land and capital goods."

"Scott!" says Helen, feigned shock in her voice. "You'd be assassinated right there."

The old man continues, unmollified, "Still I don't want to exploit anybody or to tell them what to do. We don't even own pets for that reason. We don't impose our lifestyle on other people. People should decide what to do collectively."

"Can that work in society?"

"It does work," he says enthusiastically. "There are 250 million people in Russia. They have moved up in a very brief time from being one of the most backward, poverty-ridden, disorganized societies to the number two world power. All in the span of two generations. When I first went to Russia in 1918, the streets were paved with cobblestones. They were slippery in winter and muddy in summer. The whole city of Moscow was Oriental, with mosques and superstitions. Now it's an orderly city with clean, tree-lined avenues."

"But at the expense of peoples' freedom?"

Scott's eyes light up, he pounds the table with his fist, and Helen lets out a belly laugh. The room shakes with cynicism.

"What about our freedom, kiddo!" Helen says. "Where do you get freedom? You can't have freedom in the modern world. You've got to obey traffic laws and tax laws. The whole system is regulated all over the world. What about the man who cries 'FIRE' in a movie theater when there is no fire? Can he be allowed to do that?"

"Kids today say, I want to be FREEEEeeee," Scott says. "FREEEEeeee! So what do you want to do? Drive on both sides of the street?"

"Is a dictatorship necessary in Russia?"

Scott ponders. "The less restraint, the better. But there has to be enough restraint to enable society to function successfully. I assume a dictatorship is necessary in Russia. And how have we gotten people to agree in this nation? We have a dictatorship in our courts with a gun in one hand and a billy club in the other. If you disobey the laws, you'll get arrested and jailed."

"Well, shouldn't people be happy?"

"Certainly not," Scott replies. "I haven't been happy since I saw desperate places like India. It is important to be well fed and productive, but not happy. Happiness is a state of mind between the ages of seven and 11. Then you have fun."

"Have something against fun?"

"Yeah. It's for children between the ages of seven and 11. After that, what counts are personal concerns. Social, collective, and individual concerns. Life is real. Life is earnest. You get your satisfaction by being a real and decent member of a serious society.

"The media and advertisers have exploited people in America so brilliantly. They believe that the world they see on TV and in ads is the real world. The good life. What to strive for. It amounts to so much successful pickpocketing, and the people whose pockets are picked aren't even aware of it any more. Society strives for phony values today."

"How do you feel about bringing children into this world?"

"I would be wary," Helen says. "What kind of a cheap, tawdry existence do you want to push on your kids? We live in a world of nuclear poison, junk food, and junk thought. It's not a bright future to bring your children into. As it is, we've become survivalists. We're self-sufficient here for about three months on our own. If the world tried to blow itself up again, we could live on our asparagus, chives, parsley, onions, potatoes, leeks, spinach, carrots, beets, kale, and lettuces."

"What of retirement?"

"Retirement?" Scott says, perking up. "What does it mean to retire? It means to die. Of course, if people want to commit suicide, they should have the right to do it. But there's no point to it."

"As we get closer to it, we've given some thought to death and dying," Helen says. "I hope I don't live as long as Scotto. I want a new chance in another body when I come down again. You come from somewhere, and you go to somewhere. You're here on this Earth for some purpose and should do your best. But there's no apprehension about death for either of us. Great interest instead. On we go to some new life. And we belong to a cremation society in Auburn."

"We paid $65 for the works," Scott says. "We even have a receipt. Still, in every life, society should be more peaceful, more cooperative, more just. We should all work at it. We should take a responsible interest in social problems. We should be grateful, decent, and live simply."

Postscript

MARSHALL JEWELL DODGE III was killed on his bicycle in January of 1982, victim of a hit-and-run driver. In that moment Maine lost a gentle, off-beat man who loved his adopted state and its people.

During his lifetime Dodge went out of his way to meet a wide range of people. He was drawn to things traditional and eccentric. Homer D. Babbidge, Jr., Dodge's mentor, described him as a "cultural conservationist." Always on the lookout for unique facets of New England character, Dodge gently probed to bring out the best in the people he met.

"He had absolutely no sense of time," said Robert Bryan (the Bert of "Bert & I") who first met Dodge at Yale a quarter-century ago. "He'd go off and interview old-timers in the woods and along the coast, and he'd take two days when it should have taken him one hour."

I first met Dodge during my student years at Bowdoin College. He was on campus to perform in monologue a series of Down East yarns including tales of the sea, tales of the north woods, and then a round of "good old-fashioned smut" (astutely promised for the end of the performance). By some-times winding and circuitous routes, Dodge always returned his audience to the sea. It was something he "never could get away from."

Dodge walked on the Pickard Theater stage dressed in a stylish over-coat and Brooks Brothers suit, the quintessential city slicker just off the train — poised, urbane, slightly on the shy side. Slowly warming up to a Maine accent, he took off his overcoat, took off his tie, took off his jacket — and took off his pants.

Beneath all was the apparel of a Maine fisherman from the tips of his overall suspenders to the toes of his chum boots, turned down at the tops. A black sou'wester rain hat and slicker produced out of a small valise was the icing on the cake. It was a total transformation.

[1 9 5

The master raconteur proceeded to reel off vividly-detailed accounts of the misadventures of "Bert and I," sympathetic caricatures of two Kennebunkport fishermen brought to life on a series of records.

Dodge's vision of Maine was one cherished by wealthy summer rusticators. His laconic characters were muted in humor and economic. Maine's simple Common Man often prevailed with disarming wisdom:

> " 'Excuse me,' said a city slicker up for the holidays. 'I'm lost. Do you know the way to Portland?'
>
> "The farmer lowered his newspaper and rocked in his chair in silence for a moment, considering. 'Well, you can take the old Adams Road past the Perkins' barn three miles. Turns to dirt every now and again. Keep on it straight 'til you get to a church. Turn left — two miles before you come to it. That'll get you to Portland.'
>
> "The slicker returned an hour later, lost. He said that he had found the church and followed the road.
>
> " 'Just seein' if you can follow directions,' said the farmer. 'Now where did you want to get to?'
>
> " 'Portland.'
>
> " 'Oh, Portland. Why didn't you say so?'
>
> " 'Tell me,' said the slicker. 'I passed a fork in the road and signs pointing in both directions to Portland. Does it matter which way I go?'
>
> " 'Not to me it don't,' said the farmer wearily.
>
> " 'Well, if I go left, will it take me there?'
>
> " 'Don't know.'
>
> " 'If I go right?'
>
> " 'Don't know.'
>
> " 'You don't know much, do you,' said the slicker in disgust.
>
> " 'Nope,' said the farmer. 'But then again, I'm not lost.' "

Dodge often said that there was little new in many of the stories he told. Some like *The Stove with the Powerful Draft*, capable of rocketing a log cabin to the moon, and *Gagnon, World Champeen Moose Calleur* with its transcontinental holler were traditional stories passed down through generations by guides like Ed Grant. On more than one occasion Dodge admitted to liberating old vaudeville quips and yarns from research archives and libraries.

What was new about Dodge's storytelling was his uncanny ability to master accents, mannerisms, and cultural foibles, bringing them together into eloquent and sometimes hysterical testimonials. Dodge was as skilled at imitating the nasal intercom twangs of Long Island Railroad conductors, drawling ranchers on the plains of Texas, and French Canadian fur trappers as he was in mastering the deep structure of Down East speech. He was a latter-day Professor Higgins.

There were, also, Dodge's inimitable sound effects including temperamental lobsterboat engines, eerie foghorns, and the resonating, splintering crash of Bert's *Bluebird* meeting its Maker — and the Bangor packet boat:

" *'OOOOOOOFFFFFFF!'*
" *'That were the foghorn sound of the packet, 'bout a quarter of a mile to the starboard.'*
" *'Give her another blast of the foghorn, Bert.'*
" *'AAAAAaaagggghhh!'*
" *'THAT WERE A GOOD 'UN, BERT——— but it weren't good enough.'*
" *'SCROINCHHHHHHHHHbbbbbbccccchhhhhh hh hh.'*
" *'The Bangor packet come out of the mist and struck the* Bluebird *amidships, going through her like green corn goes through the new maid.'* "

Marshall Dodge took humor seriously. He understood the complexity of rural subtlety. His stories were self-effacing without being condescending, humorous without need of belly-bursting punch lines. Audiences laughed inwardly as much as outwardly, sympathizing with the human frailties and Yankee savvy of Bert and his friend. For Dodge, the beauty in storytelling was in carrying his audience along.

Once while I was talking with Dodge in Bece Wilson's antique kitchen, he explained the difference between Maine coastal humor and that which flourished inland:

"Among fishermen living on isolated islands and narrow peninsulas, humor and the spirit of the people is contracted and subtle like their confining fogbound surroundings. Maine has been a closed traditional society for centuries. As one moves out into the forests, mountains, and into the Western prairies, land and spirit open up, giving rise to exaggeration and overstatement. You get tall tales."

To illustrate his point, Dodge told of a meeting between a Texas rancher and a Maine saltwater farmer:

" 'I don't know about your farm in Maine, mister, but I've got a ranch that's sooo large, it takes me five days to drive 'round my spread in the car.'

"Hearing this, the Maine farmer nods and says, 'Why, I once had a car like that m'self.' "

On stage, Dodge demonstrated his mastery. He was so skilled at dialect, studied pauses, and well-placed inflection that he needed no props. Like Clarence Darrow in the courtroom, the storyteller had his audience in the palm of his hand from the moment he set foot on stage until the curtains closed. Shoulders sagging, he ambled and shuffled around, hands deep in pockets, eyes heavy with melancholy. Eyebrows raised in an apologetic expression, he told even the funniest stories with a worried, almost haggard look. His facial control was supreme; he made stony-faced Buster Keaton look slapstick.

There was, however, another side to Marshall Dodge, boyish and silly. Sometimes after flubbing a story line (often making the tale even more hilarious than its original version), he would burst into giggles, shoulders heaving, face hidden in hands with mock embarrassment. Marshall Dodge, you see, was human too.

Working with Dodge was like playing with a powderkeg — one never knew when he would explode with enthusiasm. "Ah-ha! Yesss! Fantastic!" he would declare, pounding the table, laughing satanically. "Ex-cellent!"

Patron of the arts, Dodge was always ready to encourage artists, writers, poets, craftsmen, mimes, dancers, and musicians. For this book, he introduced me to a wide range of characters including Huston Dodge, Dick Shew, and Scott Nearing.

Dodge was filled with wild ideas. He once sailed a kayak from Vinalhaven to Rockport. To the chagrin of local fishermen, he used an umbrella as his sail.

Another time, he confided that he was working on an invention that would help solve the energy crisis. He would invent a four-wheeled bicycle that could be pedaled down railroad tracks. (He had a fascination with trains and had raced bicycles as a Yale undergraduate.) As a safety precaution, Dodge suggested strapping a mirror, face forward, to the handlebars; "That's so when a train is heading your way, all the engineer sees is another train. He might not stop for a mere bicycle."

Of course, Dodge's invention was totally impractical. It expended far more of its user's energy than it conserved in fuel, but such was the weird attraction of the man.

Dodge was 41 and a bachelor when he died. His creative energy found eclectic expression. In addition to producing five *Bert and I* record albums, he wrote *Frost You Say? — A Yankee Monologue* (1973) and *Bert and I and Other Stories from Down East* (1981). He frequently appeared on Maine Public Broadcasting television productions such as *A Down East Smile-In, A Fresh Breeze Down East,* and *In the Kitchen.* He was a sometime commentator for National Public Radio. His radio commercials for Maine-based companies like B & M Baked Beans, Oakhurst Dairy, and Poland Spring Water were based on the "Bert and I" motif. Attired in colorful foul-weather gear, he served as a Maine delegate to the 1980 Republican National Convention. His lifelong interest in philosophy was reflected in work on a perennial manuscript tentatively entitled *The Architecture of Philosophy.* He once said, only partially in jest, that he "would like to acquire the screen rights to Immanuel Kant's *Critique of Pure Reason* and produce it."

The culmination of Dodge's achievements, however, was the Maine Festival, "a celebration of Maine's creative spirit," sparked, organized, and partially funded by Dodge in 1977 as an annual summer event on the Bowdoin College campus.

"Artists are like Maine fishermen," he once told me. "Because they're so independent, they're impossible to organize. The best thing I ever did was to get these mimes, artists, poets, and musicians under one tent tarp."

At the end of one of his stage performances, Marshall Dodge was faced with the usual happy problem of how to stop cries of "Encore!" and leave. With a casual shrug, he hushed the audience:

"I learned my lesson of when to stop from the Coca-Cola Company. Before today's charmless plastic cans, they used to make those old-fashioned glass bottles. You know, the kind that fit perfectly into the palm of your hand.

"Well, Coke put just enough cola into those bottles to quench your thirst, except for a little which kept you comin' back for more.

"It's best to end and leave, like drinking a Coke, wanting just a little, little bit more."

The world could have used *more* than just a little, little bit of Marshall Dodge.

[1 9 9

Acknowledgments

THESE CHARACTER STUDIES AND PHOTOGRAPHS have appeared in the
following newspapers, magazines, and reviews:

Brown University Hellcoal Review
Daily Hampshire Gazette
Down East Magazine
Kennebec Review
Gloucester Magazine
Lincoln County News
Maine Life
Maine Sunday Telegram
The New York Times
The Rockland Courier-Gazette
The Times Record

Special thanks to:

James Brown, *Times Record* managing editor; for his foresight;
Judith Crist, *Saturday Review* editor;
Elizabeth Wilson for her hospitality;
Norman and Betty Pohl, Maurice and Sara Goodman, my grandparents;
Thea Wheelwright for her encouragement.
— *William Pohl*

Tom Davies and Lloyd Weller for their advice and encouragement; and to
my husband Rob, because his love and support is always an inspiration.
— *Abbie Sewall*

MILES

0   10   20   30   40   50

Subject Locations ●

NEW HAMPSHIRE

SACO R.

ANDROSCOGGIN R.

RUMFORD

M   A

Jackma

SKOWHEGAN

WATERVILLE

SEBAGO LAKE

LEWISTON

AUGUSTA

KENNEBEC RIVER

Bowdoinham

Freeport

North Whitefield

PORTLAND

Winnegance

Bath

Damariscotta

Buckspo

BIDDEFORD

SACO

Orr's I.

Robinhood

Rockport

Harborsi

KITTERY

Bailey I.

West Point

South Bristol

Owl's Head

Five Islands

Stonington

Manana I.

MONHEGAN ISLAND

MATINICUS

ATLANTIC OCEAN